WOODBRIDGE

AND

BEYOND

by ROBERT SIMPER

EAST ANGLIAN MAGAZINE LTD

IPSWICH SUFFOLK

1972

The majority of the photographs in this book came from The Suffolk Photo Survey and I am most grateful to Mr. R. G. Pratt for the help he has given me, extending to many hours.

I must also express my gratitude to Mr. G. F. Cordy of Felixstowe, who has produced some rare views of Woodbridge.

Many other people with local knowledge have given me much of their time and I must offer them my deep thanks too. - R.S.

900227   07   9

CONTENTS

ILLUSTRATIONS

CHAPTER 1

A COUNTRY TOWN

THE approaches to Woodbridge by land do not do the town justice. The best way to see it is to come by boat up the River Deben, which is a nine mile long estuary leading up from the sea; for, this way, the character of this small Suffolk town can more easily be seen.

The first thing that catches the eye is the Old Tide Mill. From this, the houses rise gently on the hillside and in the distance can just be seen the white sails of Buttrum's Tower Windmill. The slopes appear to be covered with a pattern of red roofs with green trees pushing up between them. It is a scene completely unscarred by industry. Two buildings stand out from this homely jumble of colour. One is the flint tower of St. Mary's Church and the other, the elephant grey gas works. It is, in fact, almost a typical English country town, but with enough character to remain unique. There is no other Woodbridge. Although Woodbridge has certain aspects in common with other East Anglian towns, it still has its own personality. However the name Woodbridge is not unique. There is a hamlet of this name near Shaftesbury in Dorset, another near Guildford and the place name also appears in Somerset. All these obviously originated without any connection with the Suffolk town. There is also a Woodbridge in New Jersey, U.S.A. although this is thought to have derived its name from a Dr. Woodbridge who had gone over from Dorset. However another Woodbridge in North America, this time in Canada, is believed to have got its name from our Woodbridge.

How did it all begin, what made men settle on this particular spot? The first people seriously to settle in the area were the various invaders from Northern Europe. But these Scandinavian raiders seem to have ignored the present site of Woodbridge. They chose instead to make camp on the high ground beside Martlesham Creek on what is now called Kyson Point. The name Deben suggests that it was then the Deep One and no doubt the Norsemen in their Long boats penetrated further inland, for the palace of the Kings of East Anglia was established in Rendlesham.

The site of this palace, probably no more than a group of huts, has yet to be discovered. The most recent research suggests that it lays on the land now covered by Rendlesham Forest. Certainly there is little in the hamlet now to hint of royal connections. The Kings of East Anglia did little to alter the course of events in either their kingdom or the rest of Britain, but they left behind them the burial ground at Sutton Hoo which staked their claim in history.

The world famous Sutton Hoo excavation of the royal ship burial took place in 1939 and has been described as the most remarkable archaeological discovery ever made in England. Sutton Hoo excavation took place on the open heathland on the opposite side of the Deben to Woodbridge although the barrows are concealed from the town by a 19th century plantation. There are 11 barrows or burial mounds of different sizes known as the Sutton Mounts, all of which are situated 100 feet above sea level. The most important fact is that they lay on extremely sandy soil which has enabled the grave-furniture to survive.

The mound that was opened contained the remains of a long open clinker built boat, in which the pagan Anglians had placed all the necessities they believed their chieftain would require in the next world. The most notable of these was an iron standard with the old northern emblem of royalty, the stag or hart, on a ring at the top. Another object identified with kingship was a carved ceremonial whetstone. To show the dead chief was a warrior, there were the remains of a fine shield and helmet. The most precious find was the great gold buckle of elaborate design and beautiful craftsmanship. For the chief's more immediate needs there were silver bowls, spoons, some more practical pottery and small Merovingian gold coins. But nowhere was there any sign of the body of the dead king.

The Wuffing dynasty of East Anglian Kings was founded by Wuffa, who died in 577 and ended with the death of Aelfwald in 740. All of the Wuffing line are presumed to have resided at Rendlesham, but well before they died out they became Christians. At first the Sutton Hoo mound was thought to be the grave of Raedwald, the last real pagan king and man of some importance, as he was Bretwalda, or grand chief of the English kingdoms. But Raedwald died in about 627 and relics in the mound have been identified with a christian-pagan period of at least 40 years later.

Although the subject is still open to discussion, the Sutton Hoo ship burial is now thought to be a memorial to Aethelhere. Nominally a christian, he does not appear to have had strong religious ideals. In fact, he joined the pagan King Penda of Mercia in active alliance and marched north to invade Northumbria. However the Northumbrians, under King Oswy, met them near Leeds and in the battle that followed both Aethelhere and Penda were killed. The battle lost, the army found their retreat hampered by flooding rivers in which many were drowned. This took place in 655 and presumably sometime after this the pagan element in the East Anglian Court carried out the Sutton Hoo ship burial in honour of their dead king. At this early date they had probably only learnt these customs from the Vikings of the Uppland Province of Sweden.

Woodbridge is first mentioned in the reign of King Edgar (944-975) when he endowed the monastery of Ely with the royal manor of Kingston and the lands of Ubebrycg. A track had been established from the early settlement in Kyson Point, which crossed the present site of the Ipswich road and the Fen Meadow and ended up in a newer settlement in the vicinity of the present Market Hill. This track must have crossed Steyning Brook somewhere between Drybridge Hill and the Deben. Here there was a wooden bridge from which the town derived its name.

As the manorial system developed, the wood bridge settlement became a series of small manors centred on the Market Hill. This had by then become a common meeting place. Domesday Book mentions the original Parish Church of St. Mary's. In the 12th century Ernaldus Rufus founded a small Augustinian (black) Canons Priory near the present site of Woodbridge Abbey House. This religious body acquired market rights for the little town.

At the same time as the market became established, Woodbridge began to flourish as a port. Products from the villages around were shipped out. This activity was controlled by merchants and the town began to expand. Salt making was an occupation of some importance and other crafts which have long since died out included wool combing and hat and rope making.

All this brought modest wealth to the people of the town. In the second half of the 15th century the merchants rebuilt the parish church of St. Mary in fine perpendicular style with a western tower of cut flints with freestone dressing. Later, in Cromwellian times, Dowsing and his soldiers visited the church with the aim of removing what they considered to be idols. These gentlemen did a great deal of damage to the churches in the Eastern Counties and, at Woodbridge, they mutilated the font. To those who were fond of church architecture, Dowsing was a scoundrel, but the majority of Woodbridge people at that time approved. In an area noted for its Nonconformists, the town was very much a Puritan stronghold. The town's tradesmen and craftsmen took no part in the established church and actively disliked anything faintly connected with the High Church.

Thomas Seckford was a colourful Elizabethan who managed to make his name well remembered in the town. When the priory was suppressed early in the 16th century, its land passed into the hands of his family. Seckford became a lawyer and held important official positions at the Court of Queen Elizabeth. He built Seckford Hall, which is just outside the town, in about 1560, but since this was an enlightened age he devoted most of his wealth towards helping others who were less fortunate. At the time the seat of justice was transferred from Melton to Woodbridge, Seckford built the lovely red brick Shire Hall which stands in the middle of the Market Hill in 1570. This elegant building with Dutch Gables still serves as the Sessions Hall and in the days when Woodbridge was a market town was also used as the Corn Exchange. The Shire Hall was restored in 1884 when it was briefly used as a fire station before it changed again to be the Petty Sessions Court.

Thomas Seckford's greatest achievement was the setting up of the Seckford Hospital which housed 26 aged single men. The Seckford Charities derived their revenues from an estate in Clerkenwell, London and from four streets in Woodbridge. All of these were left to the Charities by Seckford after his death in 1587. By 1861 the income from the Seckford charities was large enough to build the Seckford Almshouse in Seckford Street. The original hospital was no longer sufficient for the towns needs. Later, in 1886, the Seckford Dispensary was built and it wasn't until the 1930's that this petered out through lack of funds.

Thomas Seckford must have found his brother something of an embarrassment for the town's benefactor could not have been pleased with the knowledge that his brother Henry was a fairly successful pirate. There is no record of Henry Seckford giving money to the poor. Perhaps he financed a few drinking sprees in the towns ale houses after returning from his voyages. Once when he was master of the *Lyon* he seized the Spanish merchantman *Bonaventure* and took her into a South Coast port where he sold her cargo of wools, saffron and bacon. Such actions against the Spanish were favoured by Queen Elizabeth I and perhaps Thomas Seckford's influence at court helped to smooth out any difficulties. In 1592, however, Henry suffered a financial setback when he was fined £12,000 for taking a Venetian ship 'by mistake'.

Woodbridge still largely retains its Tudor character. Its personality is not so much in any particularly beautiful building, but in the whole homely appeal of its narrow streets which have charm that could not have been created artificially. Many of the original Tudor houses had fronts altered at a later period and in more recent years some have been swept away all together

In the early stage-coach days, the London-Yarmouth highway went up to the Market Hill and down the other side, but in the eighteenth century the Thoroughfare became the main route. This had been a residential street, but developed into the business area in between the port and the market and became the real centre of the town.

The 17th century saw the town reach the zenith of its importance as a port. Also shipbuilding was at its peak. The port was rivalling Ipswich and turning out men-of-war for the navy. The town depended so much on shipping that after the railway went through in 1859 the population dropped dramatically. The towns growth was stunted and it was left just a quiet country backwater until light industries sprang up in the 1930's.

The Suffolk coast had always been a possible place for an invasion from Europe during time of war. A garrison was first established at Woodbridge in 1750, but it was not until the Napoleonic wars that large bodies of troops were stationed here. In 1803 barracks covering 56 acres were put up on Drybridge Hill. These were to accomodate 700 cavalrymen and 4,000 infantrymen. In 1805 the 21st Light Dragoons were here. A large number of Georgian houses were built for the officers and it was probably because of them that a small theatre was erected. This seems to have given its audiences a fairly simple diet of light comedies. However the townspeople were not impressed and complained that the theatre was 'old fashioned'. In fact the people of the peaceful country market town loathed the task of quartering the red coats. The chief amusement of the healthy young soldiers was getting drunk and having a good scrap, a habit which must have placed severe strain on the tempers of the regular chapel attenders. The defeat of Napoleon was greeted with enthusiasm not because it meant the end of a tyrant, but because soldiers were no longer needed in Suffolk. The barracks were pulled down in 1815.

The 19th century saw a little group of cultured men living in Woodbridge, most of whom are now forgotten outside their home town. The first of these was Bernard Barton (1784-1849). This quiet Quaker was a clerk at Alexanders Bank (now Barclays) who wrote poems in his spare time. These poems achieved national fame and in 1845 Bernard Barton dined with the Prime Minister, Sir Robert Peel, at Whitehall. The following year he was granted a special pension by Queen Victoria.

While his poems were popular Barton was tempted to give up his work at the Bank, but both Byron and Lamb advised him against it. Neither of them were very keen on his poems, but Lamb's warning of 'trust not to the public' was no doubt a fair statement.

Instead of seeking higher fame, Barton remained in Woodbridge, seldom venturing many miles away. He described himself as having 'little more locomotion than a cabbage'. He wore plain Quaker clothes and spoke in the modest language of his religion. His habits were so consistent that housewives knew that it was time to put the potatoes on to boil when they saw the respectable bank clerk going home to lunch at his cottage in Cumberland Street.

Barton had many literary friends, but by far the closest was Edward FitzGerald (1809-1883). Born at Bredfield House, 'Old Fitz' was third son of John Purcell, who married his cousin Mary FitzGerald. After her father's death, the Purcells legally adopted the FitzGerald name and arms. Also the great wealth that went with them. As well as property in Ireland, other estates they owned were Bredfield House, Boulge Hall, Wherstead Park and Nazeby.

FitzGerald lived the life of a gentleman. He moved about a great deal, but his first home was Boulge Cottage, then for 13 years he lodged over the shop of Berry the gun maker, on the Market Hill. Finally he had the Little Grange built to his own plans, but still preferred his humble rooms over the gun maker's shop. He did not move until he had a disagreement with his landlord.

One of FitzGerald's great interests was literature and he was particularly keen on translating the classics. As a boy he had been filled with the romance of The East, by meeting Major Moor of Bealings House. This retired officer of The East India Company studied Suffolk words and archaeology. Fitz-Gerald never visited the East, but began passing away the time translating the works of a medieval Persian poet Omar Khayyam. These translations gained a great deal from FitzGerald's own poetic ability. His friends were interested in them and for their benefit he had a few printed and published in small paper cover editions. Those who read the *"Rubaiyat of Omar Khayyam"* were struck by its originality. Swinburne for instance, found a copy in a London second-hand booksellers and became enthusiastic about the transla-tions. Slowly they reached a wider public and FitzGerald's publisher was bombarded for more copies and fresh translations. The reserved gentleman of Woodbridge became a name that was known in every well read 'with-drawing' room. The Americans, with their usual enthusiasm for anything novel became particularly wild about Omar Khayyam's prophesies.

FitzGerald's other greath love was yachting. He owned the schooner *Scandal,* named, he claimed, after the chief product of Woodbridge and he enjoyed sailing on the Deben. He also took a great interest in the shipping. In 1840 he attended the launching, at Taylor's Lime Kiln Yard, of a trading schooner named after his friend Bernard Barton. At the dinner held after-wards, FitzGerald jokingly went to the other end of the room to Barton professing that he could not sit at the same table as one about to have a ship named after him. Barton's comment was: 'If my Bardship never gets me to the Muster-roll of Parnassus, it will get me into the Shipping List. . . . .I shall at any rate be registered at Lloyds.'

As a young man FitzGerald had been up at Cambridge University in the same 'set' as Thackeray, Carlyle and Tennyson. Later, on one occasion Tennyson came to see his friend. The visit was full of minor disasters includ-ing the meat being cold for Sunday lunch. However, FitzGerald took him to visit John Grout's famous stables, at the back of the 'Bull Hotel''. Grout was proud of his stud. but not particularly impressed with his visitor. Afterwards FitzGerald told him that the town had been honoured by a visit from Lord Tennyson, but Gout had never heard of him. If he had been Admiral Rous of the Jockey Club or someone as important, the honour might have been more obvious to him. Who was this Lord Tennyson anyway?

'The Queen's poet,' replied FitzGerald stoutly.

'Dis 'say.' said John Grout. 'Anyhow he didn't fare to know much about horses when I showed him over my stables.'

Everyone in the town was very proud of John Grout. Newspapers claimed that he made the town famous 'as a place where carriage and riding horses of the finest stamp could be procured'. Horse dealer Grout was the son of a small Kettleburgh farmer who had 'gone bust' at the time of the Repeal of the Corn Laws. He had worked as a groom at several inns then for Squire Sheppard of Campsea Ashe before becoming landlord of the Bull Hotel. Seven years before his death in 1887, Grout told a friend that he had sold £100,000 worth of horses in a year. The friend quickly calculated that he must have taken at least 10% profit.

'Aye,' retorted Grout 'but there are many losses, very heavy expenses.'

In an age where horses were the main source of transport, local pride saw Grout of Woodbridge in Ford of Dagenham terms. He would be remembered. And FitzGerald? Well he was a quiet old gentlemen who had a boat on the river and kept himself to himself. Few in the town even knew that he wrote, let alone dreamt that future generations would remember the town because he had lived there.

After Barton's death, FitzGerald married his daughter Lucy. This was not a love match, the couple were middle aged and FitzGerald was beguiled into believing that this was the way to care for his old friend's daughter. Unfortunately, the lady tried to force him to conform - dress for dinner and send out visiting cards. FitzGerald hated display and the couple soon parted. He remained aloof from his surroundings and spent the rest of his life appreciating the beauty of East Anglia. He mixed only with a little group of cultured men who referred to themselves as the Wits of Woodbridge. This had consisted of Barton, The Rev. Crabbe, grandson of the Aldeburgh poet, Captain Brook of Ufford Place and the lawyer Thomas Churchyard (1798-1865).

Churchyard practiced law in the local courts, but his real interest lay in painting. A capable amateur artist, his work is a poetic record of Victorian Woodbridge. Although Churchyard did a number of oils, most of his works were small watercolours dashed off at great speed as if they were studies of something to be finished later. He bought and copied paintings by John

Constable and thus developed the same style. Churchyard's art was an important link between Constable and East Anglian painting in the 19th century. Had Churchyard's heart been in his profession he would have grasped high honours and the financial rewards that went with them. But he had the overwhelming desire to paint. In 1832 his affairs collapsed and there was a sale of his belongings. Then married with five children, he left the district for a time, possibly to try his luck in London. However, he returned and lived in Seckford Street (then Well Street) and for the last 30 years of his life he lived in Cumberland Street.

Churchyard used his ability and knowledge of the law to defend the under dog. He was something of a champion of the poor and particularly disliked the 'game preservers' and their head keepers. He delighted in seeing the local poachers walk down the Shire Hall steps after their cases had been dismissed. But fate played a cruel trick on this habit. The agent of the Marquis of Hertford, one of the largest game preservers in the district, persuaded his employer to pay Churchyard a retainer as the prosecuting solicitor in all game cases. Churchyard's finances were such that he was unable to turn this offer down. It was a sad blow for the poachers.

Perhaps Churchyard was something of a poacher himself. Certainly he enjoyed a day out with a gun and dog, rough shooting. On one occasion he took his favourite retriever into the shop of the Quaker Confectioner Barritt. Unbeknown to Churchyard the dog ate a number of sausage rolls. A few days later Barritt was standing in his shop doorway when Churchyard came walking down the street. Barritt told him that a dog had eaten some of his sausage rolls.

'Oh,' said Churchyard, 'you can recover against the owner of the dog.' 'Then hand over eighteen pence,' cried the Quaker. 'It was your dog!'

'Very well,' said the quick witted lawyer, 'I charge you six and eight-pence for advice and the balance due to me is five and twopence.'

CHAPTER 2

THE GRAND OLD DAYS

THURSDAY used to be market day in Woodbridge. The Corn Exchange was open every week and the cattle sales were held on alternate Thursdays. Although, within recent years, stall holders have re-established themselves on the Market Hill, Woodbridge had lost all importance as a market centre by 1900. The organisation of large sale yards at Ipswich, and better transport, killed off the Thursday Market.

Woodbridge was the market centre for two distinctly different areas. The modern A12 road roughly marked the border. To the west lay the thickly wooded and heavy clay lands known as High Suffolk. A wheat growing area with huge Tudor farmhouses and little villages nestling in the valleys between well cultivated fields. To the east lay the sandy light lands of the coastal belt sometimes called the Sandlings. This was vastly different to High Suffolk; almost flat, it had a few trees, enclosed fields were situated on the better land but for the most part it was open and only grew 'breaks' (a dialect word for bracken). The Sandlings were frequently swept by the bitterly cold east winds (and still are). Under a huge backcloth of open sky, flocks of black faced sheep wandered constantly seeking out every blade of grass. The heath was parcelled off into areas known as Sheep Walks which supported vast flocks and the Sandlings were as remote as the Australian outback.

The 18th century enclosure acts probably did not bring as much hardship to the East Suffolk villagers as they did to those in the rest of England. Although there was a great deal of enclosing, much of the wasteland had already been taken over by individual 'pioneers', However, when the Earl of Stratford tried to enclose 60 acres of commonland at Snape, one John Woolnough brought a lawsuit against him and won. The real reason why enclosures did not upset the county was that at the end of the Viking era Suffolk had formed part of the 'Danelaw'. Here the manorial system was different. Instead of having one Lord of the Manor, each village was split up into several small manors. These, over the course of time, became small independent farms and the wasteland was gradually added to these. It is very hard to trace any large commons. The strip land let to manor tenants were often really like large allotments.

In the late 18th century most of the land was divided into farms but agricultural practices gave very low returns for the labour involved. The fashion was to grow three white straw cereal crops and then to leave the land fallow for a year. This was known as making a 'summerland'. On poorer.

land it was necessary to leave a 'summerland' every other year on this system. The fallow land was ploughed and later cultivated to break up the land and kill the 'rubbish' (weeds). This meant that vast tracts of cultivated land were unproductive and it was not until the famous Norfolk four course system was evolved that this practice was abandoned. Worked out by Coke of Norfolk, this simple system was to grow root crops or beans instead of leaving the land fallow. For East Anglia's largest industry, it was a major breakthrough.

The first golden age of farming was in the Tudor period when the thriving yeomen farmers built fine half timbered houses. Locally this meant that High Suffolk became dotted with attractive houses. The next burst was from the Napoleonic wars until the Repeal of the Corn Laws in 1843. During this time the Sandlings changed from being used for sheep grazing to corn growing, particularly barley which was in demand for making malt. The wealth of that era of agricultural well being is reflected in the local architecture. Most of the Sandlings farmhouses were either re-built or considerably enlarged in the first half of the 19th century. This boost for arable farming created a demand for more workers and many rows of red-bricked cottages were put up. These were neither exciting to look at nor to live in. Consequently the villages nearer the coast lacked much of the charm of those further inland.

Looking through the account books of the Ling family at Otley Hall, covering the period from 1745 to 1842, one gets the impression that the pattern of agriculture altered little. Everything was done by hand. I think there have been more technical advances in the last 10 years than in the whole of that 100 years. The book-keeping of these accounts had me beaten to begin with until I realised that the books had been started at both ends and worked towards the middle. These records contain bills, sales, settlements with workers, harvest contracts and Parish poor rates.

Corn was thrashed out on the barn floor in the winter with a flail, called 'a stick and a half' in Suffolk. It must have been back breaking work and no doubt if done on 'day work' too much time was probably spent leaning on the barn door discussing village politics. Therefore, nearly all farm work of that day was done on a piecework basis. The William Ling of the late 1700's paid his men 6½d a 'cum' for barley, 6d for oats and the princely sum of 1/1d for a 'cum' of wheat. These were the good old days when 'tobacco' was 1/2d a pound and a man cut an acre of barley for 1/0d.

At the time of the Napoleonic Wars prices seem to have doubled. Boys were employed much more to fill the gap by men away fighting. The boy Hammond worked a seven day week scaring rooks and crows for 3/6d.

Perhaps we can picture the boy Hammond, a cheerful but ragged urchin, tramping over Otley's heavy fields of spring corn, 'a-shouting and a-hollering fit to bust'. Few could have got much rest from this method, boys or crows, for as the boy Hammond chased them off Otley Hall, the boy Sam on the next farm chased them back again!

The farmers continued to plough up more and more wasteland, but with the Repeal of the Corn Laws the home market collapsed as soon as cheap foreign corn was shipped in. The population of the whole county continued to rise steadily throughout the 19th century, but in purely agricultural areas the population dropped from the 1840's on.

There were 620 people in Alderton, an arable district in the Sandlings, in 1844. Forty years later this number dropped by 100 and by 1921 it had fallen to 426. The same thing is true of many villages, the people just drifted away to look for work. Farming picked up sharply during the 1914-18 war, only to plunge into an even worse slump in 1920.

The worst harvest was in 1879; what a dismal year it must have been for the countryman. Three quarters of the hay and clover was spoiled, since most of it was on low lying marsh land, simply carried away by the floods. At Framlingham passengers had to be taken to and fro to the station by rowing boat.

After months of rain the harvest was begun. A wet harvest is something which has to be experienced to be understood. Days rolled by without anything being done. Corn was flattened by heavy rain, ears began to drop off. At last the weather broke and out everyone went into the fields; But not for long. Black clouds soon built up in the sky and it was not long before the first drops of rain fell. Another day slipped by.

So it was in the year that the British and Indian armies were fighting to grain control over Afghanistan. In the middle of September there were a few fine days and what was left of the corn harvest was gathered in. At 9 o'clock on the 17th September, a thunderstorm broke out, killing a cow on Dunningworth Hall marshes and another belonging to Mr. Chaptine at Sudbourne. Richard Rope of Sudbourne Lodge wanted to get his bullocks home from his Leiston marshes, but this was delayed for several days because the roads were flooded in between. Luckily he managed to get them home and yarded before the bad storms of the 23rd and 24th September.

Perhaps it is not surprising that the older generation were religious men, but there was no love lost between Church and Chapel goers. In the second half of the last century, Mr. Leggett tells us in his diaries, which he kept when he farmed with his father at Bucks Hall, Rishangles, and later on his own at Worlingworth, how he and his family went to Church every Sunday.

15

Once during a wet spring drilling he left work at 2 o'clock on a fine day to go
and hear a Mr. Hamilton preach. A month later he again left work to visit
the Church, this time to give bread away to the poor. A few days later he
drove his daughters into Eye to have their hair cut and give a cheque to
a Mr. Warner to be invested. Through reading Mr. Leggett's diaries, one can
see how fond he was of shooting. He and his neighbours had much pleasure
this way. This was the true hallmark of the East Anglian Yeomen. One
September they shot all day at Garnham's and only got one bird.

The relief of the seige of Ladysmith in the Boer War is alongside such
remarks as 'killed 8 pigs for London'. Pig killing was a monthly event on the
farm and I doubt if anybody went hungry in Mr. Leggett's household. Of
course it was much cheaper to eat food produced on the farm, fancy having
to pay 4/3d for 6lbs of beef as Mr. Leggett had to do one day in Framlingham.

Entertainment, apart from shooting, was very limited. The highlight of
the year was the Harvest Horkey. Everyone went to Church and sang 'All is
safely gathered in'. But the real climax of the farming year was the Horkey
Supper. This supper was given by the farmer to his men and was held in the
farmhouse or barn. In villages made up of small farms, everyone clubbed together. At the end of September in 1885, Mr. Leggett records going to Mr.
French's for a Committee Meeting of the Worlingworth Harvest Home Supper.
The following Sunday they had two collections for it and raised £4. 4. 1d.
The village craftsmen had their own celebration on Shummacker Monday.
On the first Monday after Christmas the shoemakers all got drunk. This
seems to have been a very local custom, the origin of which is lost.

During the whole of the 19th century estates tended to get larger and
the ownership of land fell into fewer hands. Although some of the older
and smaller estate owners lived off the rents of the land, most of the larger
ones had money invested in industry and used the returns from this to
improve their estates and maintain their high style of living.

A man who went into a London Estate Agents wanting to buy a farm
was asked what sort of farm he wanted - one for hunting, shooting or fishing?
With agriculture in a decline, the countryside had become the rich man's
playground. In East Anglia the sporting gentry made the pheasant king of
the countryside. With the same drive as they used to conquer the world,
the Victorians developed shooting— and what startling results they achieved.
Prince Frederick Duleep Singh's 17,000 acre Elvedon Estate recorded taking
a 81,877 bag in one season of which 58,140 were rabbits. On one shoot
eight guns are reputed to have shot 2,000 winged game in a day. I am
inclined to believe that a little bragging went on in the number of game taken
on rival estates. However, writers of that time defended shooting. Why, they
cried, land that could be let for sheep walks at 2s. 6d. an acre could be let for

Mrs. Berry's horse and trap in Woodbridge, 1905.

The Cherry Tree in Woodbridge, 1905.

The Bell & Steelyard in New Street, c. 1900.

The Crown Hotel, Woodbridge, c. 1910.

shooting at a pound an acre. Farming had sunk very low indeed.

In order to achieve the best results the game preservers remodelled their estates. It is no exaggeration to say that the habits of pheasants have dictated the East Anglian Landscape. Tree planting became the rage, although Fitz-Gerald complained bitterly that the new-fangled race of squires were cutting down the old woods and banks that bred violets in his childhood. This was probably simply to satisfy the age old demand for oak.

Lord Rendlesham owned some of the poorest land in the Sandlings and made the most ambitious forestry planting undertaking in the district. He started a nursery for rearing seedlings at Chillesford. Unfortunately his Tangham Forest was destroyed by fire. Later in the 1920's the Forestry Commission bought the land and re-established Tunstall and Rendlesham Forest, still drawing their young trees from the original nursery beside the Orford Road.

The Orwell Park Estate, which was most of the land in the peninsula between the Orwell and the Deben estuaries, also went in for forestry, particularly on the very light land at Nacton and Foxhall. Before passing into the hands of the Prettyman family this estate was owned by Col. G. Tomline. This estate owner might rightly be called the founder of Felixstowe because the towns growth was encouraged by him. The local story is that Tomline gave Harwich and Dovercourt the chance to elect him into Parliament, an opportunity that the people of the fashionable 'watering place' of Dovercourt did not avail themselves of.

Tomline was not at all pleased and was tempted to believe that the little hamlet of Felixstowe, since it faced south, would make a better seaside resort than Dovercourt. He was the driving force behind many of the schemes which developed the modern town along the sea front. Particularly getting the railway to the town and opening Felixstowe Dock in 1887.

Another man closely connected with many schemes to develop East Suffolk was Sir Cuthbert Quilter. Born within the sound of Bow Bells, he was the grandson of Samuel Sacker Quilter, a large farmer in Trimley. Quilter came to Suffolk for a holiday as a young man. Once when out walking he hitched a lift in a farm cart going towards Felixstowe Ferry. Here he looked out across the Deben at the barren land on the north bank of the entrance and thought that, if he ever made a fortune, that would be the place he would build a house. He did both.

Quilter became the head of Quilter, Barlfour & Co., and a member of the stock exchange. At times his financial dealings were on an international scale. In 1873 at the age of 32, he left his home in Surrey where he had commanded the 4th Surrey Rifles and moved to East Suffolk. Here he had the mansion of Bawdsey Manor built. Completed in 1882, this palace by the sea cost him £25,000 and architecturally might be described as a cross between an Elizabethan Manor House and a Maharajah's Palace. It is in a style never likely to be repeated again, but it firmly established Quilter as being a country Gentleman. Actually this industrious man could have had little in common with the older and more easy going order of country estate owners. There is a tradition that for every million he made, Quilter had another tower added to the Manor. There appears to be nine towers.

Since the aristocracy were the ruling classes, Quilter next embarked on a political career and entered Parliament as a member for South Suffolk in 1885. He was popular in his constituency but never reached great heights in government circles. He fought a hard campaign to try and bring in a 'pure beer' act. Although unsuccessful, he tried to prove his point by opening a pure beer brewery at Melton.

Quilter rarely spoke in the House of Commons and presumably he did not rise to a high position in the Liberal Party because of his bitter opposition to Gladstone's Home Rule Policy. He was created a baronet in 1906 (local legend credits him with having three times previously refused a knighthood). This came at the end of his political career as he lost his seat by 136 votes earlier in that year. He had no intention of letting the affairs of the nation pass without his thoughts making an impact. In the years after his retirement, new taxes were introduced which were aimed at the wealthy upper classes. Quilter saw quite correctly that this was the beginning of the end for the landed gentry. The taxes he was forced to pay were only a fraction of what every large privately owned enterprise has to pay today, but he felt that he was being unjustly treated and announced that the taxes ruined him, he would have to sell his picture collection in order to pay them. His taste for fine art was inherited from his father who had also been a noted collector. The Quilter collection was housed at his London home in 28 South Street, Park Lane and was sold at Christies on July 9 1909 for £87,780.

This splendid protest against taxation on earnings from individual initiative made not the slightest difference to the course of British political history. The average voter was not in the least distressed to see the proud aristocrats stripped of their finery. Over half a century passed and the whole race of wealthy with unchallenged power were made extinct before the central government began to dip deeply into the wage earners weekly packet. By then the principle of taxation on individual earnings had been long established. I fancy that Quilter, were he still alive, would only comment briskly 'I told you so'.

At its peak his Bawdsey Estate reached 8,000 acres, extending practically along the whole north bank of the Deben. This was controlled by an agent and administered from the estate office at Bawdsey. Here there were blacksmiths, wheelwrights and building tradesmen. The forestry department had its own nursery and an ambitious planting scheme. The well-known stud of Suffolk Punches kept at Bawdsey Hall, carried off prizes at all the local shows, and the flock of Suffolk Sheep won equal fame. The estate was really Quilter's private kingdom but he took his task of looking after the welfare of everyone on the estate very seriously. There was only one sin that could not be forgiven - poaching. If caught, a man could not expect to find another job the Bawdsey side of Wilford Bridge. A tenant farmer who became irritated by having the game eat his crops and ignored the gamekeepers orders to stop netting hares was turned out. Apart from these high handed actions Quilter did a great deal of good. He was the first person in the area to put up good housing for workers.

Once he passed a large group of men standing on Alderton Knoll. What, he demanded from his agent, were men doing standing about in the middle of the day on his estate. The agent explained that they were out of work. Quilter set about finding a scheme to give them employment, pits were opened on light land and the soil was sifted for flints which were used for road making.

One of his shepherd's wives, Mrs. Last who lived in the little white weather boarded cottage on Alderton Walks was very proud of her grandchildren. Quilter offered to give her a 1/- for every descendant she could name, a gesture that cost him over two pounds. Much of the estates day to day running he carried out himself. Once, at the turn of the century, nine corn stacks and the farm buildings at High House Farm went up in a glorious blaze. No one knew how the fire started but two points were clear, the tenants corn stacks were exceptionally well insured but the landlord's farm buildings were not. Quilter pretty soon went round to investigate.

'I just don't know what started it, Sir' said the farmer, standing respectfully with cap in hand. 'I just don't rightly know what I'm gonna do come next rent day. All my corn stacks are burn to the ground . . . .'

Sir Cuthbert Quilter cut him short by demanding if he used a mirror to shave with.

'Why yes, Sir, that I do'.

'Then', said Quilter crisply, 'tomorrow morning you will meet the man who started that fire.'

For all his brilliance and forceful personality there were two difficulties he could not overcome. One was the sea which in spite of £120,000 and the skill of Dutch engineers, he could not stop it from slowly encroaching on his estate. The other was the Rev. Allott Tighe-Gregory who held the living of Bawdsey Church, from 1848-1911. Quite what the original disagreements were over have been lost in the mist of time. It appears that the aged Rev. Tighe-Gregory, who used to wear a shawl, held the living until he was well over 90. He was one of those individuals who stubbornly refused to bow to pressure from strong authority. Quilter loathed him and did everything in his power to get Tighe-Gregory out. Quilter was not a man to be crossed. Once he won his point with the local education body by building another school, opposite the Star Inn, and ordering that all the children in the village went there. He tried the same tactics with the Rev. Tighe-Gregory by ordering all the tenants to go down to Bawdsey Manor Chapel, thus leaving St. Mary's parish church almost empty.

The Rev. Tighe-Gregory also held the living of Ramsholt church and every week he cycled there on his three-wheeled bicycle and gave a very short service. On one occasion Quilter and some friends went up river on *Peridot,* then walked across the Dock Marshes to church but arrived there just in time to find the parson shutting up the church. Quilter demanded that he opened the church and held another service, but the Rev. Tighe-Gregory only commented that he should be more punctual next week and climbed on his three wheeler and pedalled off.

Life at Bawdsey Manor was exceptionally rigid. Younger members of the household were not expected to speak to their elders. They had to be spoken to first. This rule was made not for servants but for actual members of the family. The winter shoots were the great social events. The Bawdsey Estate apparently used to be shot by only four 'guns', each having two guns and a loader. They are credited with often taking 400 pheasants at one stand. To achieve this the sky above the 'guns' must have gone black with flying birds.

Yet the founder of the Bawdsey Estate's greatest love was the sea. He was the Commodore of the Royal Harwich Yacht Club from 1879-1909. Yachting was then a popular pastime with the great centres on the South Coast, but was comparatively unknown in Suffolk. The older country pursuits were the ruling passion of the wealthy. Parks were very popular, Sudbourne Hall stood surrounded by over 500 acres of parkland and Ashe High House, a now demolished mansion near Wickham Market, changed hands from Sheppards to the Lowther family while Quilter was still adding to his Bawdsey Manor. There must have been talk about Ashe High Houses 144 acres of park and its famous deer herd. Bawdsey Manor had no park, only a wonderful view of the Deben flowing out into the North Sea.

Once, while on a cruise, Quilter's out-spoken habit ran him into deep water. In the Panama, he had an argument with an American. His views of the United States were not complimentary. The American passed on the opinion of a member of the House of Commons to the New York Press and the subsequent rumpus eventually got into the London papers. Anglo-American relationship was a tricky subject, but the Victorians sadly under-estimated the resources and determination of the young America. Perhaps there were some justifications, for Great Britain at that time had controlling influence over at least half the world's surface, while the Americans were still brutally subduing the Red Indians.

Another maritime endeavour was the instigation of the Bawdsey - Felixstowe steam ferry. This may have been prompted by the acquisition of Laurel Farm, Felixstowe on the south bank. Also, when the tide was not suitable to reach Woodbridge, Quilter was then able to cross and use Felix-stowe's station. The ferry consisted of two vessels which, because of the very strong tide in the Deben entrance, ran on chains laid across the river bed, In spite of this being well patronized, especially in the summer, 'the bridges' as they were referred to, ran at a loss and finally petered out in the 1920's.

An even more ambitious scheme was to transform the quiet country village of Bawdsey, into Bawdsey-on-Sea, the fashionable resort of the East Coast. This is what had happened to Felixstowe. The little village around the church of SS. Peter and Paul had been pushed into the background as an Edwardian town mushroomed up along the sea front. The Coastal Develop-ment Corporation built a new half mile long pier in 1904, complete with an electric tramway. The place was a real boom town, although the large genteel hotels along the front tried to give the image of old fashioned respectability. The town had reached the status of an Urban District by 1894, but history did not repeat itself across the water at Bawdsey.

Quilter collapsed and died suddenly at Bawdsey in November of 1911 He was then 70 years old. His estate had become a well run community, almost a miniature welfare state. The 'good and faithful' estate workers could look forward to protection in their old age and sickness. It differed from the present form of national security in that only the 'good and faithful' received this blessing. The work shy, dishonest and the poacher were not encouraged to stop in the district. Nor was there any nonsense about democracy. Quilter's decision had been final. Everyone was entitled to keep their opinions to themselves.

The social progress of the past half century has made it impossible for

any individual (unless he or she has the backing of some powerful organization) to exercise such strength. This complete change of authority is worth
drawing attention to. Today the most difficult art of any individual wanting
to put up a house is obtaining 'planning permission'. The would-be private
house owner must tread very gently not to offend the local committee or
the planning authorities. This system may allow a few horrors to get through
the net but prevents a lot more from popping up all over the countryside.
However, when Quilter had Bawdsey Manor built, he had the main road
re-routed. It was in his way.

The most famous of Quilter's family of seven was the composer Roger
Quilter (1877-1953), while the Bawdsey Estate and the bulk of the fortune
was inherited by his eldest son Sir. W. Cuthbert Quilter (1873-1952). He
lived the life of a country gentleman amidst a slowly crumbling estate. In
the agricultural depression of the inter-war years the rents of farms could not
support the grand scale the estate had been designed to run on. There was by
that time a small army of estate workers. The duty of keeping up employment in villages on the estate was still taken seriously, retired retainers were
found free housing, no one was turned away. This created a great personal
loyalty to the Quilter family, but in the long run it proved financially exhaust-
ing, Sir Cuthbert Quilter inherited such a vast wealth and benevolent power
that he must have found it almost impossible to realize that the money could
ever be spent.

Bawdsey Manor was the first sacrifice. Apart from employing sufficient
staff to maintain this small scale palace (to have not maintained it properly
was unthinkable), there was also the constant trouble with the encroaching
sea. For even after the thousands of pounds the Quilters devoted to shore
defences, the short grey waves of the North Sea still tried to gnaw it away
from the Sandling peninsula and still today the breakwaters have to receive
regular attention if the age old battle is to be won. Bawdsey Manor was
finally sold to the Government in 1936 and it was here that a team headed
by Sir Robert Watson-Watt developed radar.

The Bawdsey Estate eventually succumbed to the ravages of death duties.
The grandson of the 'right old Sir Cuthbert' Quilter, Sir Raymond Quilter
(1902-1959) was the last man to head the estate while it was intact in its
original form. Sir Raymond was a second son and was brought up to believe
that he would have to make his own way in the world, but his elder brother
died and he eventually inherited. Sir Raymond had the same dynamic personality as his grandfather and, although in many ways a very sensitive man, he
possessed the courage of a lion. As a young man he had his own plane and
also used to make parachute jumps over Felixstowe sea front to amuse the

summer visitors. The parachute was then in its infancy and although these dare devil escapades did not altogether meet with the approval from Bawdsey Manor, he later began the G.Q. Parachutes & Co. at Woking in Surrey, having rightly anticipated that the parachute would play an important part in the Second World War.

What the Quilter domain may have lost in size, Sir Raymond did not lose in originality. His home was the chauffeur's cottage at Methersgate Hall. His own airfield was on the edge of Sutton Walks and his plane is referred to as being 'the best radio-equipped private plane in Britain'. While 'in residence' at London's Dorchester Hotel he had his own standard, a golden pheasant on a red background, flying alongside the Union Jack.

CHAPTER 3

MEN OF THE COUNTRY

TO attempt to define a countryman is a difficult task. The term is only a loose one connected with an attitude of mind rather than being applied to everyone living in a rural area. Basically the countryman is part of the country. His life is set against a background in which nearly everything is growing or living and not being manufactured by any skills devised by his fellow human beings. He sees nature at close quarters and is not over-awed by it. He does not get excited about preserving wild life because he is too often in direct competition with it and knows its true force and ability to survive.

His skills are unsophisticated, but nevertheless require an alert mind. Above all, he takes pride in his achievements, whether it is high yielding crops or healthy animals. He can never afford to relax his attention if these results are to be obtained. The weather with all its fickle habits and the ever present diseases are always against him. They are formidable foes. He has to struggle hard to make sure that the seeds he plants will flourish. Countless forms of wild-life, rabbits, pigeons, insects and the rest could destroy everything and leave him with nothing in return for his labours. It is simply a case of survival of the fittest and the countryman has to be constantly on his guard.

Unfortunately too few countrymen have been skilled with a pen. Since so much of their time is spent out of doors, literature is inclined to pass unheeded. But two countrymen have stood out as being men of letters, Cobbett and A. G. Street; Neither of them had any real link with Suffolk and the gulf between them is not just time. It is a pity that more countrymen have not written. True, rural England has had its defenders, but all too often the country is portrayed through the eyes of townsmen. Villages emerge through a romantic haze as being oases of peace and basic well being. Above all there is this curious opinion that life moves slower, but in the country the four seasons come in succession and nothing will stop them. If crops are not planted at the right time they will not grow. A constant deadline has to be met. The political upheavals can shelve or ruin any system connected with manufacturing or upset the laws of supply and demand, but no one has yet succeeded in completely halting nature for a single day , although the human race has   tried some disastrous methods to try and change the course of its destiny.

One point about the countryman is certain: they were far more numerous in the past. What a tough old crowd they were, labouring away, taking immense pride in all they did. It did not matter whether it was ploughing, hedging or ditching, it all had to be done 'exact' to meet with their approval. All this gave them a great deal of satisfaction, but little financial return. The amount one man could do by hand was so limited that they could not get high returns for their labours. Their pleasures in life had to be simple and organized on a very local basis. A favourite pastime was to attend the small markets and fairs. One incident alleged to have taken place at Parham Fair in 1764 was of the man who exchanged his wife for an ox. The deal was made with a grazier and the wife was apparently quite willing. She was handed over the next day, complete with a new halter, in return for the ox which the man sold the following day for 5 guineas. This has the ring of a real country tale, spread by word of mouth until someone wrote it down The report made in all seriousness was no doubt meant to fix a price on a women's value.

These fairs were business gatherings but they played such a great part in the social life of the district that in time they became purely for amuse- ment. In one case the fair survived while the village vanished. This happened at Dunningworth, now part of Tunstall. At one time there was a church, but this had fallen into decay by the 16th century while the annual horse fair, held on the strip of ground in front of Dunningworth Hall was held right up to 1912. There would have been no auctioneer at Dunningworth Fair, the bargain would have been struck between individuals. This old practice still exists in parts of Ireland, but in Suffolk, men are no longer prepared to spend the whole day haggling over the sale of one animal. Melton Lamb Sale, held every spring on what was then a meadow beside the church, was an annual one day auction. Most of the sheep came from the Sandlings. Shepherds and their dogs set off in the early hours of the Morning to walk their 'ships' in. This sale survived the Second World War. Woodbridge Fair, at one time held on Fen Meadow, took place on Easter Monday. In 1875 it was referred to as being 'rather what used to be a fair' and was already developing into a Horse Show. By the beginning of this century it had become well known for the 'turn out' of prime Suffolk Punches. With the decline of farm horses it has lost its agricultural significance. At one time it was the highlight of the year for every head horseman, now few people 'off the farms' attend. Al- though it did not change over to exhibiting other livestock, it has happily continued as an annual showing and jumping contest which is a local event in the riding horse world.

One Blaxhall man made a living travelling round to the fairs and fighting for money. This sport, if it can be called that, lasted long after prize fighting was abolished. The dodge was to get the crowd gathered around and then challenge someone to a fight. A cap was tossed on the ground and the crowd threw money into it. The winner of the fight took the cap money. Hard old days! In the 19th century the countrymen were certainly tough, at times downright brutal.

In the Saxmundham area the gentlemen got together and formed the Association for the Protection of Property in the hundred of Plomesgate. This organisation paid 10 part-time peace officers. Sir Robert Peel's stout hatted bobbies were not established until 1829, and then only in London. In the Plomesgate Association Report for 1836 we learn something of the crime and punishment of the day. John Boom stole an ox-hide and a calf-skin from Samuel Flick at Saxmundham and was sentenced to a month's imprisonment. Robert Button took several trusses of hay from the Kelsale Rector and got six months hard labour. John Barker stole a quarter of barley at Kelsale and was sent for seven years transportation, while a man caught stealing at Leiston was transported for life.

Sheep stealing was a crime of the worst order; woe-betide anyone who was caught. A Simon Potsford of Wickham Market was accused of theft of a sheep at Simon's Cross. From here he was dragged down Draghards Hill to Potsford Wood where he was hanged. The post still stands. Whether or not he stole a sheep in the first place we shall never know. Perhaps he was a young man driven to steal to feed his wife and family. Unluckily he was caught and his sad and violent end made its mark on others.

The Plomesgate Association congratulated its members for finding more employment for the labouring classes. Which, it said: 'must tend to diminish crime. Generally speaking persons who live in idleness and have thus opportunity to organise themselves can lay plans with less probability of being detected'.

There was some justification for the lawless habits of the people in those far off days. The real root of the trouble was that work was nearly always done on a piecework basis and, at certain times of the year, particularly in the winter months, there were more men in the villages than there was work for. Later a regular weekly wage basis was established but farms and village industries still could not employ everyone born in the villages. At least then, a man could go to the town and get work, industry was expanding and badly needed manpower.

At one time villages were almost self supporting with at least a third of their population being craftsmen. The villages which bordered either the sea or an estuary provided the purely local occupation of 'marshmen'. The marshes under their care were the land which had been reclaimed from the sea, which in spite of its name was not bogland but grazing. The marshes are interwoven with ditches (never called dykes in Suffolk) which usually followed what were, before walling up, the channels in the 'saltings' i.e. land the tidal side of the river or sea wall only covered on spring tides. The marshman's main task was to watch the animals grazing during the summer. The most usual danger, especially during the dry summers, was that the animals went into the ditches after water and got stuck in the mud. Sheep were particularly prone to drowning in this way. Also cattle and colts (young male horses) often swam or jumped the ditches and got mixed up with other bunches of stock. Since one marshman had several hundred animals, belonging to different owners, under his care, careful watch had to be kept, although stray animals could be identified for a time by the tell tale grey mud on them. Since all stock, especially sheep, tend to keep moving about while grazing, marshmen did not count in ones but in twos and threes. It made counting quicker and more accurate.

During the summer months a marshman looked after stock on a large area and had to spend much of his time walking. He alone knew where all the plank bridges were over the ditches. Strangers were not always welcomed in this domain in case they left gates open and mixed up stock. In the old days the marshmen must have been in league with the smugglers but the later generations of marshmen worked alone most of the time. They liked it that way. For company, the lone marshman would have had a dog or two and perhaps, hovering in the clear blue sky above, a solitary skylark. Like many countrymen they were a race of individuals not seeking the refinements of life. Solitude gave them time to think, perhaps too much time. A Hollesley marshman used to visit the Shingle Street 'Lifeboat Inn', very regularly. He walked boldly across the narrow bridges on his way there, but coming back he played safe and got down on his hands and knees to cross.

After looking round the stock these marshmen 'made up the day' cutting thistles with scythes, a laborious operation referred to as 'scumming'. The ditches were cleaned out in the winter when the vegetation had died down. This work was done on a piecework basis for a set sum per chain and was known as 'cutting and drawing'. In more recent years Mr. Bear of Waldringfield was a familiar figure in his area, working away in thigh boots with his long narrow spades.

Most farms had a place where good reeds for thatching could be cut. These were used for barns, cottages and cart sheds. Corn stacks were thatched with wheat or rye straw in the autumn and occasionally wheat straw was used to repair reed thatch, but it never lasted as long. Old thatch was often repaired by covering it with another layer, this way it could last for up to a hundred years, provided it was netted well to keep out birds and rats. A barn at Street Farm, Bucklesham had the thatch removed in 1966 and carved on a beam was 'W. B. Thatchy 1837'. Presumably this was when it was originally thatched.

Thatched cottages were popular because they were easier to keep warm, but since the water from the roofs was caught in butts for use in the house, thatch was disliked because the water from it was black and only fit for scrubbing.

The thatcher was really a craftsman but in village society he did not rank as high as the shoemaker or the tailor. However, since stacks needed to be thatched on every farm it was a common occupation and not just specialized in by a few. In the 1890's the thatchers wages were often 30s. a week and this was certainly the highest wage earned in agriculture. Normally the thatcher had a mate working with him who pulled and carried straw.

The ability of the ploughman was probably the country skill that was noticed most. His work was on view for everyone to see and a ploughman who left the land uneven or with 'hog's troughs' at the headlands was constantly reminded of this failing by his workmates. This pride in doing a job well was the basic characteristic of the old agricultural order. It applied to all those engaged in it. A farmer was not only expected to make a livelihood from his ability to produce crops, but he was also duty bound to keep the soil 'in good heart'. Estate owners actively disliked any tenant who they thought was taking more out of the soil than he was putting back. This often meant, in their opinion, too many cash crops and not enough stock. There was a strong feeling that it was not just bad farming to try and make a maximum profit out of every acre, but it was also morally wicked. The same sort of attitude applied with those working on the farms. It did not matter how long it took to do a job as long as it looked neat when it was finished. The saying was that 'a job worth doing was worth doing well'.

Working with horses came almost as second nature. A girl of 10 who started work by leading horses at Alderton in the 1860's received sixpence a week and a shilling if she worked all seven days. Although it is impossible to admire a system which used child labour to such an extent, it is possible to marvel at the stamina of the people who worked such long hours. Ploughing and drawing (making one single straight furrow) matches were eagerly contested. In 1868 Isaac Rowe, head horseman at Winston Green Farm, won the ploughing match in that parish and received a copper kettle as first prize. But ploughing matches were only held a few times a year, normally ploughing was a solitary occupation in which the ploughman spent many hours walking up and down behind his team of horses. It was a slow process, constantly held up by bad weather. In that beautifully unspoilt, public house 'The Ship' at Levington is an iron plaque depicting two horses, a plough, the ploughman and his dog, perched on top of one of the settles. Under the plaque is the honest prayer, 'God speed the plough' which must have been uttered by many an exasperated farmer. The plough in this case is the old type widely used before Ransome's Y.L. model was introduced in 1843. George Western of Park Farm, Charsfield had until 1965 a Ransome's A.S.2 plough which his grandfather bought sometime before he moved to that farm in 1905. This was a type much favoured on the heavy lands rather than the Y.L. which had two wheels in front. The A.S. 2 simply had a skid for altering the depth of the furrow. The most interesting detail of this particular plough was that it had an oak frame, making it a survivor, in design at least, of the 18th century.

In 1934 when the Royal Show was held at Ipswich there were 265 Suffolk Horses entered, more than double the number of any other breed in the Heavy Horse Section. To have been at the Royal Show at all these must have been the best horses and there were still thousands more horses at work on the farms and in industry. By 1968 the Suffolk Punch, although not in danger of imminent extinction had shrunk considerably in numbers. At the Suffolk Horse Society's office in Church Street, Woodbridge, there were only 250 horses still registered. The Fens had become the last area where heavy horses were still worked, although several people still kept horses for showing. In Suffolk there were still a dozen studs, among them Percy Adams & Sons Ltd. of Laurel Farm Felixstowe and just outside the county W. C. Saunders of Billingford Hall, Diss still kept outstanding teams of four, six and eight horses.

Among the 19th century breeders was Alfred Smith of Rendlesham and his two sons who remained closely connected with the Suffolk Punch. Fred Smith, the Woodbridge farmer who had Kingston Hall and Barrack Farm joined the Suffolk Horse Society in 1913. Later he became secretary of this Society and held this office for 38 years. He bequeathed six acres of land including the Jetty Field to the Woodbridge Urban District Council. His younger brother Carlyle Smith farmed Sutton Hall and was a Suffolk Horse breeder on a smaller scale than Fred Smith. Like most large farmers of that day he had cast iron name plates with his name and address made to go on the sides of his waggons.

The showing of animals played a leading part in a countryman's life. It was these events that made it worth while keeping their animals in prime condition. One of the early pioneers in organizing shows was the Victorian auctioneer Robert Bond. He held the office of secretary to the Suffolk Agricultural Association for half a century and piloted its main function, the Suffolk Show, through many of its early difficulties. Born in 1827, Robert Bond was the son of a tenant farmer on the Hurts Hall Estate at Sternfield. He may well have attended the first show at Wickham Market in 1832 for his father had taken a farm in the neighbouring village of Hacheston the previous year. Mr. Bond senior wanted his son to acquire as much insight into the business life of farming as possible. There were no agricultural colleges or institutes at the time so young Bond was encouraged to spend as much time as he could with the land agent Cornelius Welton.

Welton was the first secretary of the Suffolk Agricultural Association which was formed at the White Hart Hotel, Wickham Market, in 1831. Bond accompanied him on his rounds and helped with the valuation of the large farms in the district such as Butley Abbey and Chillesford Lodge. The time spent with Welton left a deep impression on Bond, particularly the way local sales were conducted. The waste of time was enormous. Often a dealer and farmer would spend all day haggling over the sale of one cow, and then go home without striking a bargain. Spirits and wines were plied on bullock sheep and wool buyers in the hopes of softening their hearts. These frivolities took such a long time that there was little time left for the actual sale and markets had the reputation of being a drunken orgy. Bond took over the management of his father's land at Sternfield in his early 20's. His hobby became shooting and for three seasons he had the 3,000-acre Hurts Hall Estate's shoot free. Here he organized ploughing matches and drawing competitions. These were among the early events arranged by the Suffolk Agricultural Association. Early in the 19th century farm horsemen and their families lived on a diet of dumplings, cheese made with skimmed milk and sour or sharp beer. Although living conditions had improved slightly during Bond's lifetime the average horseman would only have earned 16s. a week. Few went hungry but this amount did not allow for a very extravagant mode of life. A typical prize given at the Suffolk Show during this time was 'for the labourer who had brought up the most children to live more than one year without receiving parish relief'.

When the repeal of the Corn Laws started to take effect on arable farming, the Bond family went out of business. Mr. Bond senior found a position as agent for Sir Fitzroy Kelly at Chantry, Ipswich and his son became agent at Thorrington Hall, for Colonel Benacre. To be thrown out of farming was a jolt few men got over but luck was on young Bond's side. The following year he was offered, and took, the tenancy of Kentwell Hall, a 500 acre farm at Long Melford. Sound judgment and enthusiasm soon had him firmly established in farming once more. His abilities were not passed unnoticed, for in 1857 he was elected secretary of the Suffolk Agricultural Association, and it was largely due to his drive and energy that the Suffolk Show continued to develop successfully. The East and West Suffolk Shows had amalgamated two years before Bond became secretary but the show still had many difficulties to overcome. Cattle breeders had to be persuaded to send their stock.

Even when they were in the show ring, farmers often withdrew their animals if it looked as if they were not going to win prize money. There was a protest lodged against nearly every cup winner. These situations called for a man with enormous tact who could stand firm when the need arose and Bond did not lack personal courage. In an Ipswich election campaign he once rode into a mob, was knocked off his horse and marked on his forehead for life.

The first mechanised exhibition at the Suffolk Show was at Framlingham in 1860 when steam ploughing made its debut. The show received much better support after shelter had been provided for livestock and after the various breed societies had fixed the type classifications. East Anglian farmers were very conscious of the lack of a good local breed of cattle. Bond made at least one visit to Denmark in search of better stock. This object was to supply the progressive farmers with better stock to help improve the Red Poll. These are descended from the Anglo-Saxon red cattle. The most obvious characteristic of this breed was that they had no horns, hence the name polled, and they were noted for their milk yield. When Arthur Young surveyed Suffolk in the 18th century, he recorded that Framlingham and the surrounding woodland area of the county was the home of the Suffolk Polled. A very early herd was Mr. Moseley's at Glemham Hall in the 1820's. However, there was no standard description of the breed and there was a tremendous up-roar at the Suffolk Show in 1860 when the first prize was given to an undoubtedly cross-bred animal. Controversy went on for years and the breed type specification was not really settled until Henry Euren compiled and published a Red Poll Herd Book in 1874, but it was still a further 14 years before a breed society was founded.

Two years after becoming secretary to the Suffolk Agricultural Association, Bond married Jane Beaumont of Cranmore House, Long Melford. A year later he combined his experience of farming and as a land agent and opened offices as Auctioneer and Valuer in Tavern Street, Ipswich and King William Street, London. Six years passed before he began conducting sales of cattle, sheep and swine on the London cattle markets. His friends urged him to do the same in Suffolk. He started the Ipswich Lamb Fair in 1867, Woodbridge in 1868 Framlingham in 1869, Ipswich Wool Fair in 1870 and both the Fat Cattle Club and the Sutton Lamb Sale in 1871. His firm became the largest of its kind in East Suffolk.

In 1902 Bond's son W. K. Bond, was made assistant secretary of the Suffolk Agricultural Association. Having already taken over many of his father's duties, W. K. Bond remained assistant secretary during his father's life-time. Thus Robert Bond was in his 80th year in 1906 when he reached his half-century as secretary. Bond was the main instigator who turned the Suffolk

Show from something on the scale of a village ploughing match to an annual event in which several thousands of people were concerned. He set the pattern on which it still runs today, although a show operating on a permanent site is a development that no one seriously considered in his day.

The countryman's logic was a force that could solve any situation effectively, only the methods used were not for the faint hearted. There was a Waldringfield farmer who had trouble with corn vanishing from his meal shed. Now this farmer, like all farmers, waged a constant battle against vermin, but he knew by the amount of corn missing that he had a pretty large rat to deal with. He set a gin-trap on the inside of the little finger hole of the latch of the meal shed door. This solved the problem of the missing corn, for late one night there was a loud cry of pain and surprise as the would-be pilferer gently pushed his finger into the latch hole. Whatever the man with the crushed finger may or may not have thought of this, it made everyone very respectful of the property on that farm.

In the past the battle for the minds of the people living in the country was completely dominated by religion. The contest was between the Church and the Chapel to try to draw the largest congregations. There was a very deep gulf between those who attended the parish church and those who were members of the chapel. Suffolk had a very long tradition of nonconformist worship. Although very few Chapels ever converted a whole village, they gained a foothold in most—much to the disgust of the land owning section of the community who were almost without exception keen supporters of the established Church. The labourers and their families were also usually Church goers, although they often found the public houses far more attractive. The Chapel people were usually the middle section of the community which included tradesmen, shopkeepers and small farmers. The Chapel people may have broken away from the Church of England but they were not rebels. In Wales the Chapel united the people and taught them to be great orators, but in Suffolk the effect was the reverse, it encouraged people to be modest and tended to follow the old puritan line of thought. It was always part of the East Anglian character to loathe display. Village gossip was designed to cut down to size anyone who became self-opinionated, although it was just as cruel to anyone who tried to better themselves. The country people were practical and hard working but at times a little unimaginative.

In 1864 the Evangelist church at Melton was subject to an unusual act of faith. This yellow brick building was put up by a group of Primitive Methodists next to the White House. The owner of this house - could he have been a regular Church goer? — sued the stewards of the Chapel for blocking out the light and being a nuisance to his property. In the subsequent law suit

34

Quilter's Brewery and the Coach & Horses, Melton.

Suffolk Punches at the Woodbridge Horse Show, c. 1905.

Bawdsey Manor c. 1900, before the present trees grew.

Chain ferry leaving Felixstowe for Bawdsey.

the owner of White House won the day. The Chapel quite obviously kept the light out and must be pulled down. But there was another way round this order, for if the Chapel could be moved five yards nearer Woodbridge it would be the legal distance away from an adjoining property. A firm of millwrights undertook this task, but backed out at the last minute. The Chapel stewards managed to persuade a general builder, John Cook from Grundisburgh, to take on the job. Cook strapped iron bars round the building, jacked the base up and then with five fir trees as rollers, he moved the Chapel the necessary five yards. The rolling operation took three hours and was watched by a gathering of men in stovepipe hats and women in long dresses, but one man with sublime faith sat in the pulpit while the Chapel was moved.

The moving of Melton's Chapel is an unusual case. Most of these architecturally plain places of worship lead very uneventful existances. Chapels were being built in the largest numbers from about 1860-80, and had thriving congregations up to the First World War, when the number of followers gradually dropped away until in many cases the Chapels are now being sold. How disappinted those early followers would be if they could see their hard fought for Chapels being pulled down. Men like Mr. Squirrel who left Grundisburgh in the 1820's and went over to Sutton where he devoted his life to a Baptist Mission. He held services in his cottage at first, then in a barn and, before his death in 1845, he had finally achieved his aim in having a small chapel built.

In matters of charity the Established Church was well in the lead, perhaps because it was established. The Chapels had to spend so much time raising money for   their building programme, moreover their members were drawn from the less affluent. In Woodbridge, St. Mary's Church ran a Boot Club. The idea was for those 'in happier circumstances' to give money, through Church collections, to subsidize boots for children from poorer homes. Miss Pulling, the club 'Hon. Sec,' arranged for the sale of nearly 100 pairs of boots in the first nine months of 1900. But not all charity was for such a needy cause. In the same year money was raised to give two hundred herdsmen a 'meat tea' in the grand marquee at the Suffolk Show. The Church attenders were asked to give generously as 'the expense will be considerable' and no doubt those hungry country boys ate everything provided.

Not everyone thought highly of charitable deeds; those receiving often viewed it with mixed feelings. There were often strings attached. There is a story that a Rector of Alderton at one time used to send his gardener round every Saturday morning giving soup to the poor and aged. The poor and aged, that is, who had been to Church the previous Sunday.

The Church's control over education was a very ancient right going back to the very roots of British history. When the Church began to educate the masses it started schools in many towns and villages on a 'voluntarily supported' basis, but there was not a school for everyone until the Primary Education Act in 1870. In theory this permitted only undenominational religious teaching in the Board schools, but in fact the Church retained a strong hold. The vicar went along to the school every week and gave lessons on the scriptures. Very rarely was the Chapel pastor given such an opportunity to influence the future generation. It was Gladstone, the political leader of the nonconformists, who established education for everyone. But his failure to take it out of the hands of the Church was a bitter disappointment to the Chapel people, especially in rural areas where they had no alternative but to send their children to the Church schools.

In a report of the Woodbridge Schools in 1899 the inspector made a few observations. At the National Boys School he found the boys knowledge of the Old and New Testament very satisfactory, except the older boys who omitted 2nd Samuel. Also their repetition of the Catechism was not up to the mark accepted for a town school. These unfortunate boys, who were the sole charge of the headmaster, fell into even greater disgrace over their lower standard in the use of the Prayer Book. The Girls School got off more lightly, there was only trouble over one group's repetition of the Catechism and the Infants School came dangerously near to receiving praise. Miss Kinnell and Miss Heathcote had evidently laboured hard to impart religious knowledge. But the inspector hinted that perhaps the lessons might be made a little more interesting for both teachers and children. He ended by reporting that discipline and the standard of singing was very good in all schools.

These were the days when after children had been taught the alphabet they then learnt to say it, at speed, backwards. All good practice which helped to fill in the time. History was a matter of chanting dates of the Kings of England. Although this system may not have helped people to understand the problems around them, this indoctrination of young minds certainly worked. What they were taught stuck. Even now there are members of the older generation who can quote long passages from the Bible that they probably have not seen in print since their childhood.

Most of the activities of the church were expensive and there was a constant need to encourage charity in the form of cash donations. But the Church equally encouraged other charities. In the Woodbridge Parish Magazine Mrs. Howey, Vice-President of the Ladies Association of the Eastern Counties Idiot Asylum, was gratified to report that a house-to-house collection in Woodbridge had raised the satisfactory total of £20. 2s. However, all was not quite so pleasing to the churchmen in the town. The theory of charity was that individuals gave according to their wealth. Woodbridge, in the opening years of this century had become largely a residential town, a peaceful place where people could retire and live in pleasant surroundings. The Church hinted that some of these (no names mentioned of course, but everyone living in the town then must have known who was being got at) were not digging deep enough into their pockets.

There were small expenditures such as the Choir Outing. The boys went down river to Felixstowe and the men to Crystal Palace. There were 19 men, including verger, questman, sexton and organ blower. The plea was give generously and 'therefore let it be worthy of S. Mary's congregation'. Apparently it was, at the cost of 10/- a head.

The last of the old company of change-ringers was John Fosdike, who died aged 83 in 1899. In the belfry at St. Mary's were a number of boards which recorded the various peals they used to ring. Fosdike's campanological career was a long one. He rang a dumb-peal on the death of King William IV then rang in the Accession of Queen Victoria and for 60 successive years he was one of the company which rang St. Mary's bells on the Queen's birthday — a feat which few could have equalled, but the Woodbridge Fosdikes seemed capable of doing the unusual. Back in 1753, one Andrew Fosdike, then aged 66, ran up and down the 132 steps in the 108 ft. high tower of St. Mary's seven times in 27 minutes. Quite why a man of that age should decide to rush up and down a Church tower is not recorded, but presumably he did it for his own satisfaction.

CHAPTER 4

FORGOTTEN INDUSTRIES

AT the end of the last century gold was discovered in considerable quantities in N.W. Canada. This was the famous Klondike Gold Rush which drew men and women from all over the world in a desperate bid for wealth. True, Suffolk has never seen a gold rush, indeed in many ways there was a great lack of gold, but there was once a scramble for the natural wealth found in the Sandlings. This was the now forgotten coprolite digging boom.

Coprolites are the fossilized remains of the huge pre-historic animals which once inhabited the earth's surface. The word coprolite comes from the linking of the Greek words for dung and stone - 'Kopros' and 'Lithos'. Dung stone is literally what it is . The gigantic sharks and dragon like creatures consumed vast amounts of smaller fish and animals. After this food was digested the excreta dropped to the ocean bed and slowly changed into phosphate nodules. The sharks too eventually died and sank to the bottom and their bones became phosphatised. This mixture of excreta and bones built up to a depth of 9 to 12 inches and in one of the world's great earth movements was tossed on to the surface of East Suffolk and Southern Cambridgeshire.

The first recorded use of coprolite as an artificial manure was in 1717 when its phosphatic value was discovered after it had been spread on fields at Levington by Edmund Edwards. No doubt it was used locally from then onwards, but in the 1840's the real coprolite boom began and lasted for the next 50 years. Edward Packard of Snape started the first mill there in 1843 and began to turn coprolite into superphosphate of lime which was sold as a valuable fertiliser. Packard later built a factory at Bramford, by which time other men had joined in the feverish activity and coprolite digging spread rapidly.

The beds of Suffolk crag in which the coprolite was found sometimes lay only a few feet below the surface. Enterprising contractors hired or bought land known to contain coprolite, took on gangs of labourers and sold the 'dung stones' to the mills which were opened up in Ipswich. At first contractors merely dug in the crag that was easily obtainable and then moved on but later on these places were often re-dug. All the work was done by hand and the crag was often removed in wheelbarrows. The most economic workings did not go below 20 feet deep, but in the 1880's contractors were forced to go deeper. The deepest pit in East Suffolk was one of a hundred feet deep dug at Foxhall.

There were attempts at tunnelling but these proved unsuccessful because the Suffolk crag was liable to collapse. Also the use of pit props in the shafts made it too expensive for the amount which could be dug this way. A great deal of crag had to be moved and sifted to obtain an economical quantity of coprolite. The crag was carted out of the pits in horse drawn tumbrils to the washer. Here the nodules were extracted and then dispatched to the factories for processing. Another method of extracting coprolite was to flood the workings and then horse harrow the bottom, drain off the slurry and pick up the nodules from the ground by hand. This system however, was unpopular with farmers because land flooded with slurry never recovered; It is said that even now the sites of the old washing plants can still be traced where there are unproductive areas on light land near the old pits.

Landowners naturally did not wish to have their land permanently ruined and in later digs no damage was done to the soil structure. Often it is impossible to trace where the coprolite was removed from, which is probably why the industry is so completely forgotten. The latter day method was to remove the topsoil (all still done by hand) then dig out trenches collecting the coprolite. This process was then repeated about every 20 feet when the topsoil had been replaced. I know of fields done in this way at Bawdsey where it is impossible to see any signs of the former workings. The only knowledge of it was by oral tradition.

Financial wealth was not the only kind unearthed, for countless fine and well preserved fossils of pre-historic creatures came to light. In the coralline crag S.V. Wood discovered 396 species of shells of which 144 are now extinct and many others were Mediterranean varieties which are thought to have lived in a moderately warm sea of 300-400 ft. deep. In many sections of the ordinary Red Crag unfossilised shells are common and in this crag 248 different species have been identified.

To try and date the coprolite workings is difficult. In the Woodbridge area coprolite digging began in 1845, but this appears to have been simply working the crag very near the surface. Digging in earnest in pits must have begun about 12 years later. In the 1870's 10,000 tons a year were being dispatched from the riverside quays of the Deben and Orwell to the Ipswich factories. At Levington, cottage gardens were being dug and lucky owners often obtained a bonanza of £20. probably the value of the cottage at that time. Most East Anglian Museums have a collection of these fossils, Roman remains were also found in coprolite pits. Workers were fond of finding shark's teeth, polishing them up and hanging them on their Sunday watch chains. The pit workers also laid aside intact fossils for sale to collectors.

Almost all the labourers for these pits were local men recruited from the farms. When a labourer on the land was earning 11s. a week, a pit labourer was getting up to £1 a week. This was on a piece-work basis of 1½d to 4½d per cubic yard. True, the coprolite workers had to do more hard shovelling than on the farms, but they never seemed short of willing recruits. At one time £2.10s. was obtained for a ton of coprolite and as much as 300 tons an acre was dug. Land owners no longer sold their land, but leased the digging rights to contractors. The competition was fierce and a land owner often got from £120 - £150 per acre for the privilege of having his land worked. At a time when coprolite had sunk to 24s. per ton it was costing 8s. to 10s. per ton although I have been unable to discover what the cost of transport to factories was. Possibly as much again, but this was in the 1890's when the end was in sight. At Waldringfield, where over 1,000 tons were taken from fields behind the 'Maybush' all workings closed in 1893.

The industry finally collapsed dramatically at the turn of the century. Phosphates surface mined in America and shipped to this country proved far cheaper than what could be laboriously extracted from Suffolk crag. Home producers could not compete and many contracting firms went bankrupt overnight. Some workings were left unfinished and the topsoil not even replaced. Machinery was left to rust and men searched elsewhere for work. It did not appear to create a great social upheaval as the scale of the workings had grown smaller.

There was a brief period in the 1914 - 18 war when some pits were temporarily opened and worked by machines and several thousand tons were dug. But imports started again in 1918 and these operations quickly faded out. In the 1930's some farmers reopened the pits and spread crag on their land as a cheap form of fertilizer. Apparently this was done to try and kill mayweed (the presence of which often indicates sour soil), but the spreading of crag by hand was expensive and of little use. Apart from the numerous pits which are still dotted about the Sandlings little has survived, but in the long run it has done the district good. The surviving Ipswich factories united to form Fison, Packard & Prentice, the chemical fertilizer manufacturers. This in its turn has progressed into Fisons Ltd. the internationally known business organization which brings a great deal of employment of East Suffolk. By one of those odd twists of fate the line of events has done a full circle. For it was at Levington that coprolite was first used for fertilizer and now Fisons Fertilizers Ltd. has its Research Station in the village.

Another industry which is often overlooked is malting. The process of maltings is to make grain suitable for brewing, distilling and a wide range of other uses by forced germination. Since malting barley grows well in the Suffolk climate (in the pre-irrigation days it was one of the few crops which could be grown well on very light land) the industry has always been locally important. But since maltings are often unattractive buildings, plain brick on the outside and gloomy interiors, they have not attracted much attention; although since Snape Maltings has received publicity, interest has been aroused.

Malting seems to have progressed since around 1860. Until then almost all the malting carried out was on a very small scale. As the 19th century grew older the large brick built maltings, many of which are still a feature of the landscape, began to mushroom up all over East Anglia. In the last 20 years, the old hand methods have been replaced by mechanized processes and the industry is now concentrated in fewer, far larger units.

Practically all Suffolk towns had numerous maltings. Woodbridge is reputed to have had 30. Most of them are now untraceable but there is no reason to doubt their existence for many of them must have been 'one man' maltings, simply part of an out-building of a large house or behind an inn; a reminder of the days when every landlord brewed his own beer. There are still several of the steep slate roofed kilns to be seen around the town, but the largest were Waterloo Maltings (now Ingram Smith's builder's yard) and Melton Hill Maltings (now called the Deben Mills).

Another industry which quite naturally was to be found in this great corn growing area was milling. The milling of wheat for flour is not a forgotten industry, but grinding it by wind and water power certainly is. The sight of a windmill's sails turning slowly against the background of a vast blue sky was a common sight to former generations. When William Cobbett entered Ipswich on one of his 'Rural Rides' in 1830 he counted no less than 17 mills at work. He was delighted, and from a man quick to point out faults this was quite a compliment. Enthusiastically he described them, the mills were painted white or whitewashed and the sails were black. This colour scheme seems to have been reversed later because most mills which survived into living memory were black (tar) with white painted sails.

The sight of a windmill at work held a fascination for Edward FitzGerald. There appears to have been three windmills standing on the hill behind Woodbridge in his days. Once when one of these was under threat of being dismantled he purchased a piece of land to prevent this happening. Keene wrote that this definitely made him one of the 'right sort'. But although FitzGerald saved one mill he could not save them all. When large roller mills were established at the ports with an unlimited supply of imported grain coming in, the slow stone grinding village mills were doomed.

Even in 1933 Suffolk had 64 mills working, 29 water and 35 wind. Norfolk had 60 mills relying on wind and water power and most other counties far less. Woodbridge is lucky in having one of the few surviving windmills. This is Buttrum's tower mill which was built in 1816 and repaired in 1954 by the East Suffolk County Council and the Pilgrim Trust at a cost of just under £4,000. There was also a move at one time to restore the tower mill just off Theatre Street, but the owner of the coal business and the ground surrounding it did not want intruders into his yard. Tower Mill stands on what was once Black Barn Farm and the mill was worked until around 1920 by John Tricker.

Like Tricker's tower mill, Burgh mill has also had its cap and sails removed. In this case the operation was carried out in 1934. Previously there was another mill sited slightly to the east of the present Burgh mill which was constructed of red bricks, some of which are now the Mill House garden wall. The last miller at Burgh is reputed to have kept his money under the floor and always wore a top hat when he went to market - as befitted a man of real substance.

One of the unusual facts about windmills is that they were sometimes dismantled and moved to a fresh site. Gedding mill was moved twice the last time was from Felsham in 1867. Bedingfield mill came from Oakley and Tannington mill was first worked at Framlingham.

Wingfield postmill was dragged on wooden rollers three miles from Syleham by 20 horses. This was in the late 19th century and the move was instigated by a Mr. Wingfield. This family's connection with the village is a very long one. In 1361 Sir John Wingfield built Wingfield church and a year later the College of Wingfield. Part of this still stands although the college was dissolved in 1542. In 1384 the Wingfield heiress Katherine was married to Michael de la Pole. It was this ambitious noble that became Earl of Suffolk and built Wingfield Castle, the remains of which are now a moated farm house which at one time had a drawbridge.

Even though the Wingfields lost their land they remained in the village. Indeed they are still there. The four grandsons of the man who moved the mill farm the 300 acre Lodge Farm. Their grandfather had left the mill to an aunt and she sold it to an artist Jack Penton in 1945. One of the Lodge Farm brothers, Ivor Wingfield, used to play around the mill as a schoolboy and in 1967 he bought it back and it was his ambition to restore the mill to working order.

A little nearer Framlingham is a very similar post mill at Framsden. Here Samuel Webster ground corn by 'wind and steam', the steam being the steam

Alderton Mill before it stopped working in 1932.

Details of the cap are shown above.

Regatta Day at Woodbridge, c. 1905.

Melton Street c. 1905.

Repairing the river wall at Ramsholt after the 1953 floods.

engine driving the mill when there was not enough wind. This was a common practice in the last days of windmills, but even then they could not complete as they could not produce white flour and were forced to grind corn for cattle food. Also at Framsden is a Simpers Farm which is on the Tollemache estate. An ancestor of mine was one Samuel Simper who farmed at Debenham in the middle of the 19th century. His sons eventually farmed all over East Suffolk and one of them Benjamin settled at Framsden. There seems to have been a tradition in the old farming families for the father to lend the eldest son enough capital to get a farm. Once the eldest son was established, he handed the capital on and the next son stepped out into the world.

The strong heavy land farms in the Framlingham district were ideal for wheat growing. I remember my grandfather Herman Simper, (1877-1961) who toiled for many years growing wheat and beans in Charsfield, always seemed to enquire of any farm under discussion, whether it could grow good wheat. This was an old test of land - if it could not give a high yield of wheat then it could not give a man a reasonable income. Suffolk was stuck with this theory too long, although not much could have been done to prevent it. During the 1920's and 30's rural Suffolk had a pretty thin time.. This was corn growing land yet many fields were derelict and overgrown while Gustav Erikson's beautiful square riggers brought Australian grain half way round the world to Ipswich cheaper than it could be produced locally. The plight of the unemployed industrial worker and miner during the Depression is a theme which has been written about a great deal and undoubtedly this still influences trade union thinking. But the sad case of 'over employment' in agriculture during these hard times is almost forgotten.

William Frederick Turner, my great grandfather, was not bound to any traditional outlook during this Depression. I can just remember him as a small determined man who persuaded me, a small stubborn boy, to go for a walk with him and look at some sugar beet one hot summer's evening. William Turner left his home farm in the hills near Nottingham to seek his fortune in London. His mother sent him off with a bundle of home grown food. As he walked to the station he amused himself by throwing hard boiled eggs at the telegraph poles. In the years he spent in the East End of London he was often hungry and wished he had not wasted those eggs. By the time he arrived in Suffolk he was a much wiser man, having worked up a tailoring business employing Russian Jews before selling up and returning to his first love, the land.

He settled in Somerset for a while but moved on to the eastern counties where land was much cheaper. Every Tuesday he went to Ipswich Market and often attended farm sales. Periodically he bought farms he had never seen. let alone know where they were. He acquired farms all over the place and used to set likely young men up in business - all of this gave him a great deal of pleasure but for all his enthusiasm he never made a fortune, in fact his only real achievement was not going 'bust' when his neighbours were.

When coming to Suffolk he had not reckoned on the cost of labour necessary for arable farming. In the grasslands he knew, labour was practically nil. Even though the worker's wages were then pretty grim they were expensive if the crops had to be practically given away. He is credited with having been the first man to have a milking machine in the county, on a farm near Needham Market. At one stage he lived at Home Farm, Capel St. Andrew, and had the large neighbouring lightland farm rent free for two years. This was quite a normal custom during those depressing years; many landlords had to almost bribe tenants to stay to keep their land in cultivation. On a 2,000 acre estate at Stoke-by-Nayland the rents were 7s. 6d. an acre, out of which the landlord had to pay 6s. 6d. an acre tithe. During the two years William Turner had his rent free farm, the agents were trying to find a buyer, the previous owner having gone bankrupt. In the end the agent offered the farm to him at £4 an acre which he quickly declined pointing out that he could buy all the wheat growing land he wanted for £2 an acre. However, when the agent did find a buyer offering a better price, Turner wasted no time and sold his farm as well. Real money was worth a thousand promises. After this he gave up farming, having had a difficult but worth while life being his own boss.

While the Depression stunted all progress, windmills lingered on as part of the country scene. It would have been a great pity if they had all been pulled down as soon as their usefulness was over. Rex Wailes states that the East Suffolk post mills were the finest of their type, not only in England but in the world, and fortunately one of these has survived at Saxtead Green. The first mention of a windmill here occurs in the Framlingham survey of 1309. Quite when the present mill was built is not known, but the records of one standing on this site go back to 1796. The mill house was built in 1810 by Robert Holmes and the last miller was Mr. A. S. Aldred who died in 1947.

During Mr. Aldred's time a steam traction engine was used to drive the mill when there was not enough wind. Often during the winter the traction engine was used out on the farm to drive the thrashing drums, 'throsh'en tackles' we used to call these, and after the farm men went home it was returned to the mill to drive it all through the night. It returned back to the farm again the next morning. Mr. Aldred also owned a windmill at Worlingworth and during the First World War the fan tail of this was painted patriotically red, white and blue. Saxtead Green Mill however has always been painted white and blue and very attractive it looks. Actually the old millers often referred to their mills as 'she'. Wind driven mills and ships have many things in common; both require skilful handling to prevent them from being over-powered by this fierce element. In 1951 the Saxtead Green Mill was placed in the guardianship of the Ministry of Works, has since been overhauled and is now open to the public.

Suffolk is a county of slow running streams, but this did not prevent them from being harnessed to produce power. Water wheels were put to a much wider usage than windmills, which usually only ground corn or pump-ed water. The Old Paper Mill at Bramford for instance was worked as a paper mill from 1717 to 1793 and then up to 1880 was also used for corn milling. Glemsford Mill was built in 1825 as a silk-throwing mill. Hoxne Mill was used to produce textiles, flax, linen and grind corn before it closed in 1928.

It is thought that in the middle of the 19th century there were 27,000 watermills in the British Isles. As far as Suffolk is concerned the sites of 73 watermills have been definitely identified. Although this is a large cereal growing area and naturally a centre of the milling industry, once cheap im-ported grain began to arrive at the large ports towards the end of the nine-teenth century, watermills steadily declined in number. Even in 1933 there were 29 water and 35 windmills working the county, which was slightly more than in any of the neighbouring counties. By 1968 the only remaining working mills were Baylham, Layham, Pakenham, Raydon and Wickham Market. There does not seem to have been any pattern of mill closure. Nothing dramatic happened, they just faded away.

The Bucklesham Mill does not appear to have been worked after 1930 and four years after this it was adapted to a pumping station to supply Felixstowe with water. Shottisham Mill, which in 1536 was the home of Bathelmew the miller, was worked up to 1952.

At the head of the Butley Creek stands a water mill which has been owned by the Hewitt family for several generations. The original Butley Mill is thought to have been sited some two miles further inland near Staver-ton Park and to have been moved down in 1535. The present mill was driven by an undershot wheel; that is, the water passed under the bottom of the wheel. Rarely in East Anglia were there any overshot wheels with water coming from on top, because of the lack of fall. At one stage a windmill stood on the high ground just behind Butley Mill. After this was pulled down another one was dragged by horses from Martlesham. This mill was destroyed by fire which was a common fate for windmills. The friction on the wooden mechanism being the cause. Following this in about 1890 it was replaced with a roller mill beside the watermill. Further down on the opposite side of the creek once stood a wind driven drainage pump.

Mr. Hewitt tells me that, before the First World War, barges came right up Butley Creek to a jetty 500 yards below the mill. Paul's *Eaglet* used to bring maize regularly. Mr. Hewitt's father grew lupins, which thrived on the light land and this enterprize earned him the title of the 'Lupin King'. The lupins were shipped to Belgium to be used for dye making. Much of Butley Creek is now grown up with reeds which are used for thatching.

The waters of the River Deben drove six mills at one time and the tidal waters at Woodbridge drove another one. Starting from the Deben's source little heavyland village of Kettleburgh. The mill had three 'stones', but there often was not enough water to drive them. In about 1873 a smock mill was moved from Tuddenham so that when the miller was short of water he could use this windmill. However, there must have been periods during the summer months when both mills were stopped. When Kettleburgh Mill was dismantled the wheel was taken to Shottisham Mill and used as an overshot wheel but most of the smock mill parts were taken to Parham Post Mill.

Further down there was a small mill at Letheringham. Mr. Cooper installed a small Whitmore & Binyon roller mill plant here, but the vibration shook the building so badly that it had to be abandoned. The roller mill plant was moved to Kelsale where it was installed in a gutted tower mill; but again it was unsuccessful as the machine was too far away from the prime power.

From Letheringham the Deben winds its way down between the low water meadows to the Deben Mill at Wickham Market. The deeds of this building go back to 1701, but it is quite possibly older. Robert Martin, the Beccles millwright who looked after this mill for many years, always maintained that the water wheel was of a type usually made long before the earliest deed date. This wheel weighs 12½ tons and has a diameter of 16 ft. When I visited it in 1968 it was still being worked daily and so too was the iron pit wheel which was installed in 1880. This is typical of the slow moving gears of a mill, they seem to have rumbled on for decades, requiring little attention .

The Deben Mill had sufficient water to be worked for 24 hours a day except perhaps during a very dry summer. However, it was once run in conjunction with a four common sailed windmill. This mill was pulled down in 1868 and the bricks were used to build a steam mill. In 1885 the milling business was taken over by Ruben Rackham and he put up the Deben Roller Mill, about 40 yards east of the watermill, to take the record harvest of 1893.

The steel roller method of milling wheat was perfected in central Europe in the 1860's and when later introduced into England the traditional stone grinding system was doomed to extinction. It is an odd twist of fate that the Deben Roller Mills ceased to work first in 1949, while the watermill continued in use.

The Deben Roller Mill was driven by a steam engine manufactured by Whitmore & Binyon, which was a local firm which had its head office at 64, Mark Lane, London. Their machines all proudly bore the address of their works at 'Wickham Market, England'. The engine which went into the mill when it was built is 25ft. long and has a 9ft. 6in. flywheel. Since being taken out, its owners have very kindly presented it to the East Anglian Museum of Rural Life at Stowmarket.

The milling business was operated by E. R. & R. T. Rackham Ltd. whose activities were not wholly confined to grinding corn. The watermill was still worked because of the interest taken in it by Ruben Rackham's two sons Edward and Robert Rackham. Seventy five year old Edward Rackham began work at the Deben Mill in 1910 and he was the only man left who knew how to work it. The flour ground there was sold to local bakeries Although the mill had three stones, each 'stone' weighing 8 cwt., only two stones were worked at once. Edward Rackham was told that the three stones used to be worked all at once, but this had never been done during his time. He believed that it would throw too much strain on the great crown wheel. This massive wheel has 120 wooden cogs which were renewed in 1927. Mr. Rackham lived in the house on the end of the mill and did not get iron cogs because they would have made too much noise.

A little further downstream is another mill which the Rackham's were connected with. This was rented by Ruben Rackham and later the Rackham brothers worked it for three days a week and the owners, Loudham Estate, worked it for the other three. Edward Rackham always knew it as Ash Mill, he worked this until 1956 when it was preserved. It never had any other power except water, an unusual feature was that it could be driven with only 2ft. of water at the sluice gates.

The name Ash Mill was probably used by the millers because it was simple to say, but it was also referred to as Campsea Ash Mill, was Ash Abbey Mill and quite recently Loudham Mill. The original millwas built by the Austin Canons of Campsey Ash Abbey, which was founded before 1195. The remains of this priory are near Abbey Farm House and here in 1843 six stone coffins were dug up. The remaining two mills which stood on the Deben have both been turned into attractive houses. Both were quite small mills, the one at Ufford ceased to work in 1916 and the last miller from

Melton Mill moved to Ipswich in about 1896.

The Tide Mill at Woodbridge is one of the most unique industrial buildings in Britain. It has had a long career spanning nine centuries of usefulness. It must have provided flour for many generations of people living in the town. The first mention of the Tide Mill was in 1170 when the canons of Woodbridge Priory granted Baldwin de Ufford a plot of land so that he could have easy access to the mill. These early records do not state the type of mill, but since no possible alternative site has been found for de Ufford's mill, it is assumed that it stood in its present position. This is the first known record of a tide mill in the British Isles.

Before reclamation, the Deben must have reached further inland. Station Road must have originally been a track just above the high tide mark. Presumably a medieval quay reached from the Boat Inn to the Tide Mill. At that time a small stream which started in the grounds of Woodbridge School flowed down across the Thor'oughfare down Brook Street and ran out into the Deben on the southern side of the Tide Mill. In 18th century prints the course of this steam can still be seen coming out near the mill. The stream is now piped but originally it must have washed away silt and kept the berths open. The present Ferry Dock must have been developed to provide suitable places to discharge cargo as ships grew larger.

The mill was an important part of the local economy and in 1436 Sir Robert Willoughby granted it to the Priory. At the dissolution of the monasteries it returned to the ownership of the crown and in 1564 Elizabeth I granted it to Thomas Seckford. It is thought to have remained in the Seckford's possession until 1672.

No evidence has yet been discovered accurately to decide when the present four storey structure was built. The most likely period is in the second half of the 17th century. At this time shipbuilding for the Royal Navy was flourishing in the town. Another interesting old structure is the steelyard which was used for weighing corn and still stands beside the 'Bell & Steelyard' inn in New Street. The steelyard was erected in 1674 and it may well be that the Tide Mill dates from roughly the same time, although Kenneth Major, who has made a scaled drawing of the mill, found what are believed to be 18th century ship timbers in it.

The workings of Woodbridge mill do not differ from an ordinary water-mill. The difference lies purely in that the tidal water was trapped in the pond on the in-coming tide and used to drive the mill during the following ebb tide. Some tide mills had ponds which were also fed by fresh water, but at Woodbridge the mill relied solely on its seven and a half acre pond of salt water. The work done in the Tide Mill was of course tidal and once the flood tide had covered the ferry hard there was not sufficient fall of water to turn the wheel. The mill had four stones. Although there is said to have been enough power to drive all four at once, only three ever worked together during the last years that the mill functioned.

In a map of 'Town and Port of Woodbridge' drawn by Isaac Johnson in 1827 the mill and its granary appear to be just as they have survived until recent years. A little later the premises were owned by George Manby and worked by John Benn. The machinery was then valued at £258 and the tenants fixtures at £41.

A photograph taken in the 1860's shows a white weather boarded Tide Mill and granary. * Alongside the quay, two tops'l schooners were discharging. No doubt at first only local grown corn was ground at the mill, but by the end of the 19th century imported wheat was being brought here. When A. Hayward & Son traded as corn merchants from here they expanded the business by building a steam mill where there was a reliable supply of water, opposite the gas works. There was then regular barge traffic bringing up wheat, although the flour was not taken away by water after the 19th century. Arthur Thorpe, who as a young man worked as a docker, known as a 'humper' at Woodbridge, recalls that barges were unloaded by a gang of six men. The operation was carried out by hand, two men down in the barge's hold, two men on the winch lifting the sacks to deck level and two men carrying sacks on their backs up a plank to the second storey of the granary. They reckoned to unload a barge in a day and a half. It is doubtful if any wheat was brought in by water after 1926.

In about 1932 the Tide Mill wheel began to give trouble. The existing wheel had been put in by Collins of Melton some 80 years previously. A new wheel was built on the old shaft by Amos Clark. This millright was closely connected with the mill during the last years it was in operation. Amos Clark was born in 1875 at Weybread and his family owned land at Debenham. He learnt the trade of a millright from his father, the secrets of this craft having been handed down successively from his great-grandfather. As a young man he worked in London, but during the First World War he brought his family back to Suffolk. He established himself at Woodbridge and looked after Tricker's, Buttrum's and the Tide Mill. (Mills seldom had names but were known by the men who worked them). Just at the end of the war he moved to Charsfield and then to Parham. Here he had the blacksmith's shop and also owned the Mendlesham Post mill, which was worked by his brother George. Next Amos Clark moved to Grundisburgh and while he was there he pulled down Mr. Nunn's mill.

After the war there was a great shortage of seasoned oak, which was in
* See East Coast Sail by Robert Simper, Published by David & Charles.

demand for putting the face on mock Tudor houses. Amos then employed up to eight men and during the following two decades he pulled down over 80 wind and watermills in the Eastern Counties. This must have been a sad task for a man whose real vocation was to repair them. Fortunately not everyone wanted their mill destroyed, it was a job that could only be done once. His knowledge was in very great demand by the time of the Second World War as there were by then few craftsmen able to look after the remaining mills grinding by stones.

Apart from the Tide Mill wheel, another of his accomplishments was the construction of a huge pit wheel for the Duke of Grafton's Sapson watermill in Buckinghamshire. This was in about 1942 by which time Amos had settled at Belle Vue Road, Ipswich. He built the Sapson wheel in his tiny back garden. The neighbours were most intrigued as Amos's handmade masterpiece took shape. At the time his family were not impressed, as the operation ruined the garden and it caused quite an upheaval when the wheel had to be taken apart in sections and carried through to the road to be loaded on to the lorry.

In 1950 he repaired the famous Pakenham Mill near Bury St. Edmunds. This is a fine tower mill and had been damaged in a gale two years previously. Amos restored it to working order with full sails and went on working as a millwright up to the end of his 78 years. All his four sons were apprenticed to his craft, but later went into other occupations. The last to carry on the family tradition was his younger brother George Clark. The two brothers had worked together for many years. During the 30's they had moved an attractive post mill from Aldringham to Thorpeness where it was used as a water pump at the seaside holiday village. The Aldringham miller hated to see his beloved mill being dismantled so the Clarks used to work on it when he was at Chapel on Sundays. When they re-erected it they put a half crown under the post for luck.

The A. Hayward & Son enterprises seem to have prospered. They expanded with branches at Leiston and Walton near Felixstowe. However their steam mill shut down in the 1920's and from then on the business was confined to Woodbridge. Mr. Hayward took Geoffrey Le Mare Atkinson into partnership and later he took over the business. Until the Second World War there was nothing unique about the Woodbridge Tide Mill, it was part of every day life, but after this it became obvious that it would be the last survivor of its kind. A survey finished by Rex Wailes in 1938 revealed that there were 23 tide mills left in Britain, of which only nine were then being worked by water. There had been tide mills at Dunwich and Ipswich, both of which had long since stopped. The Walton-on-the-Naze Mill was pulled down in 1921 and the post-mill beside it collapsed the day the demolition of the tide mill was completed.

Woodbridge
Tide Mill
February 1968.

Sailing barge
'Herald' leaving
Woodbridge c. 1911.

Norwegian timber brigantine at Kyson Point c. 1904.

Top sail schooner off Ferry Dock, Woodbridge, c. 1905.

A better known Essex tide mill stood at St. Osyths and worked until 1930. After being derelict for years it was blown down in 1962. Another at Fingringhoe straddles the creek and additional milling buildings have been added to it so that it remains useful, though it has long ceased to function. Maldon seems to have had one at Mill Beach but all traces have gone.

I believe that one of the Cornish tide mills ran until after the Second World War but after this Woodbridge was the only one working in the British Isles and the whole circumference of the North Sea. In 1950 a preservation scheme costing £500 was carried out with the support of, among others, the Suffolk Preservation Society. Again the wheel began to give trouble; the original shaft was by then over a hundred years old. In the following summer the wedges which secured the wheel fell out and floated away on the tide, while the wheel continued thrashing around in a drunken fashion until it was stopped. More frequent causes of damage were through children throwing wood into the mill pond. Some of this driftwood got through the sluice and knocked the paddles off the applewood wheel. This meant that Jack Hawes had to drive into Ipswich to collect Amos Clark so that he could put the damage right.

In 1954 A. Hayward & Son was bought by the Witnesham farmer John Matthews and he modernised the plant and installed a diesel engine in the Tide Mill. Using water power was too elaborate to survive any longer. It had meant that grinding could only take place a few hours each side of low water and this meant working at least one night shift. The time had come when a dusty miller was no longer required to tend the gently rumbling mill by the soft light of an oil lamp on a cold winter's night, while the wind screamed around the old time worn mill. The tide that came creeping over the mud and lapped round the footings twice a day went unheeded. It was all finished.

CHAPTER 5.

SHIPS AND SHIPPING

THE details of the first established trading centre at the entrance of the Deben estuary are shrouded in mystery and it is probable that the true facts will never be known. The riddle that many men have attempted to unravel is whether the Roman fort Portus Adurni stood guarding the Deben mouth. The Roman colonies in southern England were constantly attacked by savage Norsemen. To guard against these marauding pirates a chain of forts were put up from Porchester to Brancaster. The construction of the forts was under the command of the Count of the Saxon Shore, and they were all apparently completed by the death of Constantine in 337 A.D. Nine of the forts listed in the Litus Saxonicuns, which was drawn up in 428, have now been accurately identified. Only the site of Portus Adurni is not clearly known, although there is considerable reason to believe that the lost stronghold stood on the south bank of the Deben.

The culprit for the uncertainty is the encroaching sea. Every storm for centuries has eaten away a little more of Suffolk's sandy coast. All that remains of Portus Adurni is now on the sea bed, just to the south of the present Deben mouth. The next known fort in the chain to the north is at Burgh Castle near Yarmouth and to the south, 'Othona' at Bradwell in Essex There is also evidence that a considerable settlement was situated in the Felixstowe area in the 3rd and 4th centuries and that it was lived in right up to the end of the Roman occupation.

Long after the Roman civilization had collapsed a castle was built at this probable site. In this case there is no doubt of the castles' existence. In medieval times much of Norfolk and Suffolk came under the domination of a powerful and aggressive family called Bigod. The first definite record of them is in 1101 when Henry I granted Framlingham Castle to Roger Bigod. They acquired further favours from King Stephen who, sometime before 1153, granted them an earldom. The title later used by the Bigod's was Earl of Norfolk, although they were also entitled to call themselves Earl of the East Angles. Having gained control over such a wide area the Bigod's began to take part in a power struggle which revolved around the crown.

Framlingham Castle was the centre of their domain but they also held Bungay Castle and controlled the Sandlings from Walton Castle, which is recorded as being built in the north-east angle of an old square Roman fort at the Deben mouth.

In 1154 Hugh Bigod deserted King Stephen for the young Henry who, when he became king, gave Bigod more privileges. But the new king soon, quarrelled with his powerful East Anglian subject. In 1173 Bigod made a mistake and backed the wrong side. He joined forces with the king's rebellious sons. A group of loyal Suffolk knights seized Walton Castle against Bigod. Possibly they saw it as a way of breaking Bigod's stranglehold of the country. The Earl of Leicester landed with a band of Flemish mercenaries and attacked Walton Castle. This was held for four days by 22 soldiers under the knights Gilbert de Sanford, Roger Esturmey, William Vis-de-Leu, and William Tollemache. Being unsuccessful, Leicester made off to Framlingham and joined up with Bigod's forces.

Henry II succeeded in crushing Leicester's army. Bigod had already attacked and plundered Norwich, but quickly made his submission to the king. Henry however took the opportunity of clipping Bigod's wings and ordered the destruction of Framlingham and Walton Castles. Bigod's strength was still formidable and Henry had Orford Castle built between 1165 -1172 in his own name at Orford. The Castle then overlooked the entrance of the river Ore, which has since moved some four and a half miles to the south.

Even in 1722 there were still remains of the old Roman fort although sheep grazed where Walton Castle had stood. In time, the sea devoured this land. In spite of the loss of its castle the Deben entrance still remained a place of considerable importance throughout the medieval period for this was the vanished Suffolk port of Gosford. There was never a place of this name, the term was used to cover all the creeks and landing places in the lower half of the Deben estuary. There were no sea walls then and the Deben must have been a fine wide expanse of water. The name Gosford is Anglo-Saxon and it is presumed that the geese frequented the ford which was probably situated at the head of the Kingsfleet Falkenham. Anyone travelling from inland to Walton Castle passed this way.

The Bigods encouraged the growth of Gosford but, after their scuffle with the king, Walton became a royal manor. The site of Manor house is now under Felixstowe Town cricket ground. Both Edward I and Edward III stayed at Walton Manor and in times of war assembled fleets at Gosford. Gosford sent 13 ships and 303 mariners to fight for Edward III at the siege of Calais in 1346. In return for this service they were granted the right to supply Calais with beer and provisions. In the following century the men of Gosford were voyaging as far as Iceland after cod.

For all its ancient and royal connections Gosford was doomed to extinction. Ships preferred to go up the estuary and discharge at the growing market town of Woodbridge. By the 17th century all traces of Gosford had

61

gone, although the name still appeared on very early maps. The saltings were enclosed to create grazing marshes, Kingsfleet silted up and where the little 3-masted 'Crayers' had once ridden at anchor, reeds grew and there was only enough water for swans to swim in.

Woodbridge had its share of the lucrative wool trade. The industrious Tudor merchants made sure that the place expanded. The first Custom House was erected on Woodbridge Quay in 1589, but sometime at the latter end of the next century it was moved to Quay Street. By then the port was thriving; the annual revenue on Suffolk cloth alone amounted to £2,722.

With Woodbridge shipping expanding the Port began to come into its own as a shipbuilding centre. The main reason for this was the forests of prime oaks growing on the heavy land of High Suffolk. Ships were doubtless built here in Tudor times, but the 17th century saw an enormous demand for timber, especially in the Thames shipbuilding yards. But transporting such ungainly logs proved a major problem. It was easier to build the ships at Woodbridge than cart the timber to the Thames. The first people to bring this piece of logic to a conclusion were the Pett family. Trading ships of note were being built before they took an interest in Woodbridge but, once the Petts gave their support, things expanded rapidly. The Petts were extremely numerous, possibly originating in Harwich, but by the 17th century they were well established as shipbuilders on the Thames, mainly in the king's service. In 1599 Phineas Pett became master shipwright of Deptford where he built the *Prince Royal,* 55 guns, in 1610 and between 1635-37 the famous *Sovereign of the Seas.* These were then the finest ships afloat anywhere in the world and no doubt there was a great deal of Suffolk timber in both of them.

While on timber buying expeditions in Suffolk, Phineas Pett often lodged at Thomas Cole's Crown Inn, Woodbridge. He eventually arranged for his fifth son Peter Pett (1610-1672) to marry Cole's daughter. The marriage took place in 1633 and through his wife Peter Pett gained property in Woodbridge which included the Crown Inn and Lime Kiln Dock.

Between 1625 and 1638 11 ships of substantial size were built in Woodbridge, the largest of which were the *Levant Merchant* and *Muscovy Merchant* both, of 400 burden tons. The *Prosperous Mary* built about 1635 was taken to Deptford to be rigged and later came back to load 171 tons of provisions at Woodbridge Town Quay for the army in Scotland. Peter Pett became Master Shipwright at Chatham and later as Navy Commissioner was allowed to give contracts for the building of men-of-war. He saw to it that some of these went to Woodbridge: Thomas Adams, Edmund Munday and William Carey all got much sort after contracts.

The first ships built for the navy were the 4th rater *Advice*, 544 tons, 230 men, 48 guns, and *Reserve*, 513 tons built at Woodbridge in 1650 at a cost of £6-10s. per ton. The practice was that after the vessels were launched (the *Reserve* drew 15ft. of water) they were towed or sailed under jury rig to the Thames for fitting out. The builder appears to have been under contract to supply the ship partly manned. Local men however were not keen on the navy and preferred to serve in the Ipswich colliers where, even if the pay was bad, at least they received it.

Adams had trouble finding enough workmen to finish the frigate *Maidstone* and when she was completed he had to take command of her, The Dutch were then doing all they could to stop the coastal shipping and often large fleets of merchantmen lay in Harwich harbour. The *Maidstone* was employed guarding the coast after a Dutch frigate had chased a hoy into Woodbridge Haven. A hoy was a passenger carrying vessel and the Woodbridge Haven is still marked on some maps at the Deben entrance.

Even if the Dutch wars caused a great demand for naval vessels, Woodbridge as a coastal town bore much of the burden in Britain's struggle for maritime supremacy over the Dutch. Munday travelled to Woolwich to try to obtain the money owed for some timber he had sent. In 1653 General Blake landed 300 sick men with orders for them to be cared for by the people of Woodbridge. The arrival of these meant higher taxes for local people to support them. Many of Munday's and Carey's shipwrights promptly fled from the district. The town already had Dutch prisoners on its hands and it had also incurred heavy losses in a law suit against the Seckford family over the almhouses and trust money, all of which amounted to the town being in debt by £500.

While Oliver Cromwell remained lord Protector, much attention was paid to the strength and general efficiency of the navy. In 1654 the 4th rater *Preston* 516 tons was launched at Woodbridge, just a year after the *Maidstone*. On the restoration of the monarchy in 1660 many ships were renamed; *Maidstone* became *Mary Rose* and was finally captured by the French in 1691. The *Preston* became the *Antelope* and was sold in 1693. The Woodbridge ships served the navy well, although at times their masters appeared to have used them as privateers rather than for any high minded ideals of being instruments of national security. Only Edward Russell, who at one time was master of *Reserve*, rose to high rank. This colourful admiral destroyed the French fleet at La Hogue for which he was created the Earl of Orford.

On the announcement in 1660 that Charles II was to be made king, the bells were rung in St. Mary's, Woodbridge. One man, however, still spoke well of the protectorate and was promptly taken before the magistrates and was ordered to keep good behaviour. At the time of the restoration steps were taken to make the measurements of ships more accurate. Since Elizabethan times general confusion had grown up around the method of classifying ships by their tonnage. In theory the term 'tons burden' described the amount a vessel could carry. The reformed system of 1660 still only gave a rough estimate which made vessels on their tonnage measurements seem smaller. Therefore Woodbridge built ships such as the *Darling* of London 350 tons, *Resolution* of Aldeburgh 300 tons, and *Protection* of Ipswich 200 tons were in fact a good deal smaller than their tonnage suggests. Another case is the *Goodman,* built in 1634, which is described as being 700 tons, but she would not have been nearly the same size as a modern motor coaster of that description.

There was no lack of work for the town's shipwrights. From 1630 to the end of the century 15 men-of-war were launched here, and repair work was also done. While *Centurion* was being repaired in 1658 her bowsprit broke and six men were drowned. In 1666, when the plague swept through the town killing over 300 people, the frigate *Albermarle* was launched. It must have been a difficult time to complete a wooden ship. The labour requirements were enormous; every piece of wood had to be sawn by hand.

In the spring of 1968 I saw a replica of a ship similar to those built at Woodbridge during the 17th century. This was the *Nonsuch* being built at Appledore in North Devon. The first *Nonsuch* was built at Wivenhoe, Essex in 1650 and 18 years later she voyaged to North America on charter to the Hudson's Bay Company. It was this company that ordered a replica of her to be constructed for their 300th centenary. The *Nonsuch* is 53ft. overall while all the Woodbridge naval vessels were (if all recorded information is correct) over twice the size. The amount of timber that went into the vessel was fantastic compared to the modern wooden craft. Treenail fastenings, not modern bolts, were used in the construction of the replica. The yard concerned was using all efficient power tools, yet it took about a dozen men nine months to complete *Nonsuch's* hull and spars.

Although Woodbridge was near a plentiful supply of oak the lack of water must have made launching a large ship difficult. Certainly Harwich and Ipswich began to take the lead. Also Peter Pett ran into deep political troubles. Following the custom of the day he gave the lucrative state offices to his near relations. His enemies would no doubt have done the same, but in the end they had him thrown out of office. However the town's reputation must have been quite good, for the building of warships did not quite end with Pett's dismissal. In 1675 the largest vessel ever built on the Deben was launched into the little tidal estuary. This was Edmund Munday's 4th rater

Kingfisher 663 tons. Later she took part in the capture of Gibraltar and ended her career as a hulk at Harwich. The last warships from the town's yards were the 5th raters *Hasting* and *Ludlow* both 381 tons and 32 guns, built at the closing years of that century.

There is a description of the town in '*Suffolk Traveller*' written about 30 years later:

'Here are two Quays the common Quay and where the chief Imports and Exports are, and where the fine "Woodbridge" salt is made, and above this is the Lime-kiln Quay where formerly the Ludlow Man of War was built. Some years hence another Dock below the Common Quay, where the Kingsfisher Man of War was built, but this is now (cut) from the River by a mud Wall and almost filled up."

The 18th century is something of a blank as far as Woodbridge maritime history is concerned. The town remained a port and shipbuilding centre, but few records of that time have survived. The only ship yard was the Lime Kiln yard and this then covered the strip of ground running from the Deben right up to the Thoroughfare. Timber was stored at the top end and the ships were constructed where the Lime Kiln Road houses now stand. The actual Lime Kiln stood on the ground between Gladwell Dock and Sun Wharf. This area's connection with the timber trade lasted until the 1920's. for little Scandinavian square riggers used to bring cargoes to Messrs. Brown's yard which then occupied what is now the down river end of Robertson's yard. Like all the deep draught vessels which visited Woodbridge, the Norwegian brigantines had to discharge part of their cargoes into lighters at Kyson Point.

Shipbuilding has always been a precarious occupation. In 1751 Edward Darley went bankrupt, although his property included the Boat Inn and Anchor Inn he was apparently building at the Lime Kiln yard. Samuel Turner took over and built ships as well as being a timber merchant. In 1764 he built a 240 burden ton ship for the Jamaica trade. This was the largest built in the town after the men-of-war, but the capital outlay must have been too much for Turner. Perhaps the buyers did not honour their agreement. Bad debts can ruin any organization. But whatever happened, Turner went bankrupt not long after the ship had left the Deben.

The next builder of note was William Dryden who came to the Lime Kiln in 1796. He produced a number of vessels for the coastal trade. Some of his bigger vessels were the 150 ton brig *Britannia* and the packet *Henry Freeling* (Capt. P. C. Mason) which was used on the Harwich to Holland passenger and mail services. Some of the brigs could only carry 100 tons of cargo but for all the dangers in their trade they must have paid their way

65

quite quickly. The 180 ton brig *Union* was built in 1815 and went back to the Lime Kiln yard for major rebuilding 16 years later.

In 1818 Dryden sold the yard because his health had given out. His retirement was short as he died in the following year. The yard had been taken over by William Bayley who launched a 'fine cutter' and a brig within a week of each other before the end of the year. In 1820 he performed the unusual feat of launching the Schooner *Commerce* fully rigged.

About this time William Garrard re-established the yard at the Common Quay. This area is now known as the Ferry Dock and even then Garrard's was sometimes referred to as the Dock yard. He was responsible for the schooner *Mary & Betsy*, sloops *Sarah, Hope and Lark* and a six oar galley 'for gentlemen to row'. Later William Garrard & Son of Brook Street were boatbuilders and shipowners with controlling shares in the sloop *Sportsman* until she was sold to the banker Fredrick Alexander and at one stage they also owned the *Hebe* outright.

Bayley seems to have expanded the Lime Kiln's capacity, but not everything was a complete success. He attempted to launch the *Bessie* with 150 people standing on deck; the schooner fell over on the slip, but was 'saved' and later successfully floated into the Deben. When the *Fame* was launched in 1824 Bayley had three other schooners on the yard in various stages of completion. This schooner like many others was for Mr. J. Cobbold. Unfortunately the Lime Kiln Yard did not offer enough scope for the ambitious Mr. Bayley and he moved to Ipswich where he was undoubtedly one of the few to make a modest fortune in his calling.

Dryden's son, W. H. Dryden took over the Lime Kiln next in 1826. The same year saw the launching of the 120 ton *Elizabeth*, which must have been the last brig completed there. Another of W. H. Dryden's vessels was the curiously named schooner *Countess of Coker* and the sloop *Mary Ann* which was 'christened' by a small girl of the same name, but after only three years the yard was up to let again.

William Taylor took over in 1830 and his shipwrights continued to meet the demand for coastal tonnage with a long stream of tubby little schooners. Not all of them for ownership in the town. *Albion* was acquired by Southwold interests and *Grecian Daughter* went to Manningtree. The keel was laid of another schooner for the same owners on the day she was launched. Ship building was then thriving in no uncertain way.

In the first half of the 19th century the two masted tops'l schooner was the most common rig used for trading vessels on the Suffolk coast. The single masted vessels were 'sloops'. Their rig is what is now known as gaff-cutter.

66

During this time there was an average of about 30 schooners owned in and trading fairly frequently to Woodbridge. They were certainly no clippers, but round bowed, with a pronounced tumble home and square stern. Their appearance was solid and plain, they had no figureheads and the only decoration was the name in white letters on the bow. Their purpose was to make a profit for their numerous shareholders. Their voyages took them where ever profitable cargo carrying work was available in European waters.

In one January gale the sloop *Cumberland* was driven ashore at Southend, the schooner *Mary & Betsy* put into Ramsgate with her bulwarks washed away, and the *Hebe* was caught by the gale in The Sound between Denmark and Sweden. Both her anchor cables parted and the schooner would have been driven ashore if a boat from H.M.S. *Thunderer* had not reached her with another anchor and cable. Not all hazards were caused by the weather though; in 1842 three schooners at the Common Quay were broken into. A gallon of whiskey was lost from the *Thetis* and the entire stock for a forthcoming voyage was stolen from the Yorkshire built *Bee*.

The best known Woodbridge schooner was the *Bernard Barton*. Her modest claim to fame does not entirely rest on the fact that she was named after the famous poet, for this stout vessel appears to have out lasted her contemporaries. Before her launching on 21 April, 1840 at least 23 other schooners had been completed at the Lime Kiln yard in the previous 40 years and nine followed her in the next few years. The *Bernard Barton* 82 tons is registered simply as a schooner but sailors would have called her a tops'l schooner as she had two square sails on the fore mast. Originally steered by a long tiller she was typical of the little ships then being built.

A vessel is traditionally divided into 64 shares. The shares of the *Bernard Barton* were owned by William Trott 24, Cutting 16, two Sutton men, one a miller and the other a farmer had eight each and her master Edward Passiful had the remaining eight. Her voyages appear to have been between Liverpool and her home port. Presumably the schooner's main function was to bring oil cake round from Liverpool in the days before the railways came into being. Just after the railway finally reached Woodbridge the *Bernard Barton* was laid up at Lime Kiln Quay with the sails taken off the spars.

The last schooner built at Woodbridge was the *Ellen* in 1853 and she sank off Yarmouth 22 years later. The *Gleaner* was broken up and the *Thomas* cut down to a lighter. At the same time the Sunderland built *Sylph* was hulked, while the *Kate* sank in the North Sea. But some schooners were sold to fresh ports and eked out a living for a few more years. The *Friendship* went to Colchester, and the *Brothers Friends* to South Shields. The *Bernard Barton* was sold to the West Country. In 1851 William Trott had paid £120 for a fourth share in her at an auction, although he received a good deal less when she was sold. The old schooner was taken to Poole in 1862 and lengthened. The usual method was to saw the vessel in half and add some to the middle. After this she became a ketch registered in Gloucester. In 1893 she was owned by Thomas Ridler and presumably worked to Porlock and Minehead. She finally sank off Lundy Isle in 1899 while bound to Cardiff from Chichester with a cargo of wheat.

Going to sea was one of the ways a man could better himself in those far off days. The way was open to any capable young man to rise to command a schooner. Most of the masters also held a few shares in their vessels and in many cases they eventually became shipowners. The most successful at this in Woodbridge were George and William Trott of Castle Street. Several vessels were registered as being under the ownership of Trott & Co. but in fact they only owned a percentage of the shares and acted as managers. These two master mariners held over half shares in the *Mary & Betsy* which was built at Woodbridge in 1827 and finally wrecked off Holyhead in 1865. They managed the *Alexander* too until she sank while on passage from Middlesbrough to Ipswich, taking her crew down with her. Since the banker of the same name also held shares in her she was presumably named after him. Then there was the *Perseverance ex - Ellen Catharionon* which was sold to Grimsby in 1852, but had originally been a prize. The other schooners registered to Trott & Co. were *Harriet, Flora, Laura* and *Richard & Sarah,* all built in the town and often trading to Liverpool. Also there had been owned in the town the sloop *Liverpool* until lost in a gale during 1840.

Woodbridge could then have been called a sailing ship town. Although several miles from the sea, maritime activities touched on almost everyone's lives. The way in which capital was raised to build the schooners meant that most tradespeople were involved. Shares changed hands quite frequently; a schooner probably spent 40 years trading to the town with her owners changing constantly. The master mariners held a highly esteemed position in local society for it was on their ability that the town prospered. Also there were mates, seamen and boys who manned the schooners, the shipwrights who were always patching them up. There were two sailmakers at the Common Quay, also rope and twine makers. A Swedish and Norwegian vice-consul and a ship agent to deal with the handling of cargoes.

The town was the port of registration for all vessels owned on the rivers Deben and Alde. At one time there were 70 vessels totalling 5,000 tons registered here; however the customs duty collected showed a decline as the century grew older. In 1834 it was £2,263 for the year, in 1844 up to £4,315, then nine years later down to £1,565. There was still over 20,000 tons a year 'going over the quays' at Woodbridge, but all was not well in this small Suffolk port. Ship building stopped, a new source of timber had been made available to the world. This was from the Canadian Atlantic coast. Local business men began taking the opportunity of using this in the 1850's and they acquired the brigs *Archibald,* 246 tons, *Bredaldare* 95 tons and the brigantines *Wallace* 123 tons and *Antelope* 156 tons, all were products of Nova Scotia and New Brunswick yards.

Getting schooners and brigs up to Woodbridge was a difficult laborious task, to say nothing of coming in over the dangerous bar at the Deben entrance. Handling the clumsy schooners in confined waters meant frequent delays. Loaded schooners required 10 to 11 feet of water and there was often not sufficient water for them to get along side the quays.

Probably the greatest drawback to the schooners was that they had to be ballasted to sail safely when no cargo was available. This meant that, after discharging coal, 40 tons of ballast had to be purchased so that the vessel could be sailed back north for another freight. At Woodbridge, sand was bought at three shillings a tumbril load and this the master sold in the northern port, probably just covering handling charges, but this process cut down the vessel's earning time.

These heavy rigged little schooners had a bad habit that worried the town's conscience. They often sailed off into the cold grey North Sea and did not come back. There were no schooner hulks rotting in creeks, some were broken up for firewood, but most of them were destroyed by wind and sea. In 1820 the sloop *Sarah & Caroline* ran on the Newcome sand in a gale. The hull sank and the crew of five took to the rigging. Luckily the Lowestoft Lifeboat reached them before they collapsed with exhaustion. The nine men on the schooner *Constant Trader* were not as fortunate when they ran on the Cork Sand a month later. Again the crew went up the rigging but conditions were so bad that no vessel could get near to take them off. Eventually the power of the waves and flying spray tore them off and one by one they fell into the sea.

Over the years the ships of Woodbridge met their end as they went about their normal occupations. The *Clementina* got ashore on the Goodwin sands during a gale in December 1884. Everyone on board including the owner was drowned. *Dorothea* met a similar fate on the Haisbro sand. The *Maria* foundered off Cromer while others like the Norwegian built schooner *Ariel,* one of a number of schooners and cutters owned by Whyard of Orford, and *Archibald* were simply 'lost at sea'. They just never arrived at their destination.

The loss of men at sea and the hardship it caused their families could not pass un-noticed in a small community. In 1840 a group of local maritime worthies met at the Anchor Inn (now the Station Hotel) and formed a society to give financial aid to the relatives of drowned seamen and compensate for any personal 'gear' lost. Known as the Woodbridge Shipwreck Society it lasted for nearly 70 years and in 1870 it had a reserve of £1,600. Most of the money was collected through donations from wealthy residents. The society had 163 members and the business was carried out by a voluntary committee. George Trott was one of the founders of this, so too was J. Dowsing, master of the *Dispatch,* and Mr. Loft the boat builder.

Claims to the society varied, aid was given to relatives of Will Marsh, who drowned after falling over the stern of the *Bernard Barton* and to Charles Bridge's people after he was killed by falling from the tops'l yard of the *Harriet* while the schooner was off Southwold. These men's relatives received pensions but when George Pannifer was drowned while bathing off the Portugal coast in 1886, the committee did not think that this was strictly within the ship's duty and his father only received half the normal compensation.

Quite a number of men came to grief in the shelter of the Deben estuary. Thomas Jackson was drowned off Kingston Quay when his punt upset as he was going off to the barge *Phoenia.* A seaman from *Flora* was drowned at Waldringfield; he had put the master ashore and was going back in the boat alone. Most schooners carried five hands and the committee 'expressed their strong opinion of the dangerous practice of permitting only one hand to accompany their master ashore unless they be furnished with two small oars'. Presumably the drowned seaman had been sculling the boat, which, in spite of the strong opinion of the Shipwreck Society Committee, still remains the normal practice on barges and small coasters.

All too often the committee had the duty of paying compensation after shipwrecks. The *Thetis* (Capt. John Bull) was wrecked in the Humber, while *Bee* (Capt. William Woodruffe) struck the North Pier at Sunderland during a S.E. gale. Capt. Woodruffe survived this, only to be wrecked at Tees in the *Mary Ann.* The *Charlotte* was lost in the great gale of 1860, while the *James* sank at Harwich when on passage from Grimsby to Woodbridge with salt. The *Harriet* founded on Dyck Bank off Dunkirk.

John How, master of the *Garland* was paid £4 for the loss of his charts 'destroyed in the dreadful gale time they were cutting away her masts in Drumore Bay'. It was a hard life combatting the sea in small wooden sailing vessels.

CHAPTER 6

SAIL TO THE END

THE population of Woodbridge in 1801 was just over 3000. The town prospered and by 1851 the numbers had risen to over 5000, then suddenly they began to drop. There was no future and the people began to move away; however, the coming of the railways stabilized the situation and the population remained much the same until the 1930's. When various light industries grew up in Woodbridge the population began to increase again. Thus in 1959 when the *'Woodbridge Reporter'* celebrated its centenary, the town's population was almost the same as when this newspaper was established.

There had been an earlier newspaper, the *'Woodbridge Advertiser'* started in 1843, but this had only appeared every four weeks. The *'Reporter'* was very much more up to date as it was a weekly; it must have been born on a wave of optimism for it began the same year as the railway reached Woodbridge. The history of the railways is really part of the national development, it ended the town's importance as a self-contained unit.

In 1794 one coach a day and a weekly wagon passed through the town on the way to London. The coach took 13 hours to reach its destination but this situation had very much improved by 1844 for by then 12 coaches, omnibuses, carriers' wagons and carts passed through the town each day on the way to London. To travel from Woodbridge to London then took five hours and it cost 10s.

The railways did not meet with everyone's favour. There was a slight commotion when the East Suffolk Railway bought the Lime Kiln area in 1856. A man named Smith was running a boat yard where the Cinema now stands at that time. This was all swept away and so too were the ancient salt pans where salt had been extracted by evaporation. Possibly the reason for having the station just near the quays was really because it was easier to get the track level on the flat ground next to the Deben. When the railway started in 1859 many people believed that this was the end of the town's usefulness as a port. But in fact shipping went on for another 60 years and it was the road transport that dealt the knockout blow.

The shipowners and master mariners of Woodbridge must have watched with guarded enthusiasm as early locomotives hauled lines of loaded trucks into the station. As they walked home from Chapel on Sundays they must have discussed the situation in low tones - could they compete with those horrible hissing engines which dragged goods into the town? There was by this time a new kind of craft being used in the Thames estuary, spritsail barges, which first began visiting the town in the 1850's. The local men were not impressed - 'ditch-crawlers' they called them. It was better to stick with schooners than got to sea in sailing lighters.

In 1883, 346 sailing ships and three steamers brought 22,968 tons to Woodbridge, which did not indicate a decline of its importance. Two years later there were 219 vessels registered here but the majority of these were Aldeburgh and Orford craft engaged in fishing. Woodbridge registered craft gave employment to 350 men and boys. The people of Woodbridge began to lose interest in the port, which was after all only a few tarred weather-boarded warehouses standing on simply constructed quays overlooking a muddy little estuary, which half the time was just a wide expanse of mud with a few swans paddling around.

The sailing barge, both spritsail and ketch rigged 'boomies' quickly came to dominate the East Coast Ports. Over the years they brought and took away thousands of tons from Woodbridge, yet very few were owned here or had local men as their skippers. George Collins of Ramsholt told me that his father and uncles, like man men from coastal villages, went off into deep sea square riggers in the 1880's and 90's. These seafaring Collins liked to get about; one was in a clipper on the Australian run, George's father spent a time in the S. Pacific Isles on a trading schooner. After each voyage they went back to their families in Suffolk. As I write, there are two ship models hanging on the wall above me. Presumably these were made to help while away the off watch time as the clippers ran back from Australia.

One of his uncles, also a George Collins, went 'a-bargin' and became mate on a boomie trading more or less regularly to the German ports. He brought a wife back from Germany on one trip and set up home near Sun Wharf. It cannot have been a soft job taking a flat bottomed barge across the temperamental North Sea for a living. The owners split the freight money with the crews, yet boomie mate Collins only averaged 15s. a week and had to get parish relief to bring up his family.

Old mariners were justified in calling early barges ditch crawlers and mistrusting their ability to make sea passages. One of these local barges was the *Bengal* of Woodbridge. The dry facts that have survived about this vessel are that she had a topping bowsprit and was built at Ipswich in 1857. In the autumn of 1967 I took the ocean racer *Giselle of Iken* away from Snape Quay. 'Jumbo' Ward had just brought *Gillation*, 250 tons up with the first imported freight in recent years. He then piloted us down river, and the conversation turned to barges owned by Newson Garrett; *Bengal* had been one of these.

Jumbo Ward's grandfather, one 'Ducker' Ward, went to sea at the age of nine in 1859, on the *Margaret*. This 35-ton cutter was engaged in carrying ammunition from Hamburg to British ports. Once, while on passage from London to Snape, young 'Ducker Ward' shouted to the skipper that there was a whale on the Buxsey sand. The skipper shook his head - 'No boy, that's no whale, that's a barge's chine'. Sure enough it was one - the *Bengal* in fact, floating bottom upwards, and all her crew had been drowned. Apparently when she had been built, money had been tight and the yard owner had laid off his workers, but as he was bound to pay his apprentices he got them to construct the *Bengal* 'on spec'. Unfortunately the lads turned out a barge which was wider across the bottom than at deck level. The *Bengal's* career was comparatively short - her stability was always doubtful.

Probably the first barge owned in Woodbridge was the *Maria*, 22 tons (not to be confused with the *Maria* which sank off Cromer). She had been built at Ipswich in 1832 and was sold out of the Deben in 1845. This barge probably had leeboards, but was cutter rigged. The first spritsail barge must have been *Phoenis* built at Maidstone in 1840 and acquired by a Woodbridge timber merchant. Next came the 43 ton barge *Eltharn* built on the Thames and this was probably only one step away from a sailing lighter. She was purchased outright by master mariner Jeremiah Read of Crown Place. Whatever her sailing qualities were, the little *Eltharn* did not have to waste money on ballast and was not held up getting up the upper reaches of the Deben. She no doubt earnt the money which was later invested in better spritsail barges.

In 1862 the *Eltharn* was sold to Maldon owners and Captain Jeremiah Read took over the *Lady of the Wave*. This was a true 'spritty' and traded regularly to Woodbridge for many years. By 1892 she was owned by Alf Bayley of Ipswich but her name appeared in the Deben pilots' records until 1909. In some of the later records she is actually referred to as having been built at Woodbridge, but the early records give her place of construction as Ipswich. To add to the confusion, there was also a Brightlingsea barge of the same name also built at Ipswich.

In 1874 Captain Read and the merchant G. Ling had the round sterned *Deben* built at Ipswich. This was the second craft at least to bear this name; another one was a sloop built in Holland in 1846. The barge *Deben* was steered with a long, rib tickling tiller and then later by a wheel. She served the town as a hoy running regularly to London and bringing back mixed cargoes. Another hoy was the 50-ton ketch *Hope*. It is remembered that she brought cans of paraffin and other household goods. In 1891 the *Deben* was run down by a torpedo boat in the Thames. After being raised, she was sold to an Ipswich shipowner, John Baker, and finally to Paul's. Three years after the *Deben* was built, Read had the *Lady Ellen* built at Ipswich, and his sons later skipper owned these barges, Frederick having the *Deben* and Arthur the *Lady Ellen*.

During the first half of the 19th century, Woodbridge had had a vigorous maritime community revolving around its fleet of schooners, but this interest in shipping just melted away. Jeremiah Read and, later, Robert Skinner were the only men who attempted to build up a fleet. If Woodbridge is compared to the Essex sea port of Maldon (these two small towns have a great many aspects in common) one finds a vast difference. At a time when the only barge registered as being owned in Woodbridge was D. Jackson's *Arthur James* (and she does not even appear to have traded to the town!) Maldon had 100 barges on its register, over 50 of which were owned by merchants and skippers of that town. Much of the Deben's water traffic was taken over by the Essexmen. They had the enterprise to build barges especially to trade to very shallow creeks. The Essex bargemen looked on both the Deben and Alde as being 'nothin' more than big cri'cks', although the same criticism could be applied to some of their own estuaries. Maldon's success was largely due to the fact that it specialized in supplying fodder for the London carriage horses and they began loading freights of straw and hay in such places as Kirton Creek, Hemley Dock and Stonner Quay. The lofty mast, sprit and red-brown sails of the sailing barge was a familiar sight towering above the grass covered river walls.

In the years before the First World War the Barges of Clement Parker of Bradwell dominated the Deben. Not only had the Essexmen taken over shipping, but also the fishing. Originally it appears there were Woodbridge smacks, small cutter rigged craft working in the estuary only, presumably supplying the towns limited need for fresh fish. The last of these was Peter Broom's tiny *Jim Mace*. Woodbridge men also used to go fishing and 'eel bumping' in lugsail boats. These small open boats were even fitted with fish wells and the live fish were later stored in fish chests off the Jetty.

The Deben fishery was on a very small scale and not really large enough to provide a living wage. (There was longshore fishing from Bawdsey and Shingle Street, but this is really another story.) Quite when the Essex smacks first took over the Deben is not certain - it could have been a very old practice. Every summer four smacks worked by the Stoker and French families came round from West Mersea. Judging by the photographs, the smacks appear to have been about 30ft. long and were very suitable for working in confined waters. At weekends the smackmen went home leaving their smacks anchored off the Ferry Dock near the station. A favourite haunt of theirs was working from the tide mill up to Melton Dock, trawling for eels with very fine mesh nets.

74

Loading Barges, Waldringfield.

Loading a stackie barge for London at Waldringfield, c. 1890.

Cement works at Waldringfield, 1897.

Children's outing from the Ferry Dock, c. 1908.

Warehouses at the Ferry Dock, c. 1905.

It may seem surprising that men who lived some 40 miles away knew that there were eels off Melton, but at that time the Essexmen were visiting the fisheries all round the British Isles and they left little worth having behind them.

Half way down the Deben at Waldringfield stood Frank Mason's cement factory. Mason originally bought an old lime kiln and the quay, but saw better prospects in manufacturing cement by baking chalk and Deben mud. When the factory was in full swing it had twelve kilns (kells, to give them the usual Suffolk pronunciation). Mason acquired seven sailing barges, *Petrel, Elsie, Bertha, Jumbo, Augusta, Excelsior and Orinoco*. These worked the 'round trip' taking cement to Ipswich, oilcake to London Docks, for export, and then returned to Waldringfield with Chalk or coke from Deptford Gas Works. A steamer, the *Winifred*, was on an almost regular charter running cement to the north of England. At times, as much as 400 tons a day was loaded at Waldringfield. The atmosphere on the quay was one of sweat and dust.

In 1907 Mason began another factory at Claydon and the one at Waldringfield was closed down, although it took five years to dismantle the factory. Most of the barges were sold to Cranfield Bros. and the last of these working was the *Orinoco*, until she was run down by a collier in the Thames during 1966. Another link, however, with the only real barge fleet the Deben ever possessed lasted a little longer, for Mason's barges all had a white moon on their topsail and Cranfields adopted this emblem. Their last sailing barge *Spinaway C.* still carried the 'moon in her topsail when she was sold to become a cruising barge yacht in 1967.

Mason's factory had been supplied with mud by the stumpy barge *Kingfisher*. Two men used to take her and drop down river just below Waldringfield; they then loaded about 25 tons of mud by hand from the saltings. in one tide. There is a tradition that one of the reasons that Mason's moved away is that some authority forbid the removal of the mud any longer. This is about the only dredging the Deben has ever known. The river at Ipswich has been extensively dredged over the years, and even Harwich had its channel greatly deepened. There was one early attempt though to try and improve the approach to Woodbridge in 1879. This was the cutting of a channel through the saltings so that vessels would not have to use the difficult Troublesome Reaches. The Woodbridge bookseller John Lodger was sued by a school teacher for libel and had to pay £100. The town's people, however, felt that there had been a slight miscarriage of justice and raised £250 but Lodger declined this offer and gave the money for the cutting of a channel to help improve the town's trade.

All trading vessels took two pilots to reach Woodbridge - one over the

Deben bar and the other from Waldringfield up to Woodbridge. These men were official pilots, not 'hufflers' (men who could be hired to lend a little local knowledge and manual labour to help the barges up difficult places). The records of the pilots at Bawdsey Ferry give a rough guide to the amount of shipping. In July 1879 seven pilots earned £39. Twenty three years later in the same month, six pilots earned £31. The shipping was practically all barges and they entered the estuary at the rate of 15 - 20 a month. They stayed for anything from four days (which must have been the quickest a barge could get up to Woodbridge, discharge and come back down to the entrance) to two weeks. All Parker's and Mason's barges were trading regularly at this time, and so too were *Thames, C. &. W., Cygnet, Frederick William* and *General Jackson*. Others that came fairly frequently were the *Spinaway C, Waveney, Sportsman, Norseman, Alde, Ethel Edith* and *Sussex Bell*. Craft which made occasional visits included *Sara, Saltcote Belle, Shamrock* and *Pacific*.

Spritty barges were sailed up here whatever the direction of the wind, but the boomies' gaff rig was a handicap and they were 'worried up'. The boomies brought coal from the northern ports to Sun Wharf and Hart's Dock (Part of the old Lime Kiln quay now known as Gladwell's Dock). For a return freight they loaded a mixture called 'mill wash' which was used for road making. Once the *Eastern Belle* got aground across the channel here and 'broke her back'. This must have been a harassing place to bring a boomie. One barge mate named Tricker Finlay, thoroughly depressed by having to pole his boomie into such a berth, swore that 'may this dock fly a-fire afore I ever come here again!'. He was knocked overboard by the boom off Harwich and drowned during the following trip, a fate that made his prediction correct.

For all the difficulties, the boomies were trading to the town until after the First World War. The 90-ft. *Reindeer* used to bring coal to Hart's Dock and load trees back to Gateshead. Once in Goole she sat on her anchor and later on passage in the North Sea, she foundered with the loss of all four hands on board. Often the boomies followed the old schooner practice of loading shingle at the Deben entrance or round at Landguard Point. This was sold in the north for the construction of wharves and docks;

The *Sussex Belle* brought what was probably the last cargo of coal to Sun Wharf, Woodbridge, from Alerton Main in about 1923. Surprisingly, there was still one tops'l schooner frequently seen in the small ports of Suffolk; this was the *English Rose*. Once, many years ago, the *English Rose* was wind bound in Yarmouth Roads and her skipper 'wired' for his girlfriend to come up from Dover. While she was travelling a fair wind sprang up, but the schooner stayed at anchor while the rest of the south bound fleet sailed on.

At last the girl friend arrived and the *English Rose* continued her leisurely way to Dover. Here the girl friend's sister came aboard and the skipper took a fancy to her and invited her to share the aft cabin. The result was an almighty row between the sisters, and, in a great frenzy, the original girl friend threw herself overboard. She was followed closely by her sister, but neither of them could swim. The skipper jumped into the boat and managed to save the sister. After the inquest, the skipper and sister were married on the same day, and they sailed off on the evening tide towards the north for another load of coal.

When the *English Rose* came to Woodbridge, she had to have 30 tons taken out of her at Sutton Ferry before she could get up to Lime Kiln Quay. Her skipper was then Jim Lewis who was later master of the boomie *Laura*. Once when anchored at Ramsholt he walked to his home at Boyton, leaving two Shottisham boys on the barge. That night the boys stoked up the fo' c'sle fire and turned in for a good night's sleep. Both being sound sleepers, they did not hear a westerly gale spring up; what with that, and a spring tide, plus the fact that there was not enough chain out, they woke to find the barge high and dry up against the saltings. When Skipper Lewis returned he had some very hard words of practical advice to give his crew. Not that it made any difference for the barge had to stay there for a fortnight until the next spring tide when she floated and continued up to Woodbridge.

A man who 'ran away to sea' in the days when every tide carried a barge up to Woodbridge was Arthur Hunt. He was the son of Sir Cuthbert Quilter's head gamekeeper and, unknown to his parents, signed on in a boomie which was discharging coal at Ramsholt Dock. After this he went on up to Woodbridge in the barge to help them finish unload. Arthur's parents walked six miles to plead with him to come home. In the end, after all the arguments over the follies of a sailor's life had failed, they bought him sufficient clothing to help him on his way. Later, he went into Parker's barges, first as a mate and then briefly as skipper on the *Dover Castle,* and also went as one of the racing crew on the *Violet Sybil.* Following a disagreement with Clem Parker he left and joined the Fowey schooner *Alert* at Ipswich and voyaged to Newfoundland. During the First World War he went into steam ships, but after a lung injury, returned to his home estuary, the Deben.

Arthur acquired a philosophy of a man trained in sailing ships and developed a considerable talent at spinning a yarn. He was the last professional yacht skipper on the Deben in Captain Gilbey's *Genesta*. In the winter, the *Genesta* was laid up against the broken down barge quay and Arthur made nets in the cabin for Aldeburgh fishermen and week-end trawlermen. I spent many hours during my school holidays sitting in the cabin listening to yarns about the 'old days'. He was glad of someone to talk to as he worked.

away at his trawls in the snug little cabin. His face was weatherbeaten to a walnut colour but the top of his forehead where his cap went was always white.

One thing Arthur did give me was his father's recipe for poisoning rats. Now the parish always seems to have suffered from an excessive number of rats and I had long heard of old keeper Hunt's ability to kill them with a secret mixture of which he would never divulge the contents. What I was solemnly presented with was a very faded piece of paper on which a Norwich chemist had written a reliable rat killing bate, back in the 1880's. It had been treasured by the Hunt family until, as there were no longer any game-keepers in the family, it was passed on to me. I was very flattered but never dare put Hunt's poison into action. It started off harmlessly with 'one peck of fine barley meal sifted,' but the real knock-out ingredient is capable of killing every living creature for miles around.

How I wish that I had written down some of the stories that Arthur Hunt told me. Perhaps the best tale was that of the fate of one of Mr. Bloss' bullocks. Around about 1912 the *Pacific,* one of Goldsmith's of Grays barges was laying in Melton Dock when its skipper and mate discovered that they had developed that recurring human phenomenon - they had spent all their money. Perhaps this was a common occurrence for this pair - perhaps they could not get a 'sub' from the owners. In this unhappy state, they sat on the barge's forehatch with nothing else to look at but a bunch of Mr. Bloss' fat cattle grazing on the marshes.

Now the mate of this barge had at one time been a butcher's assistant and he must have been the prime mover of that night's dishonest work. They drove a bullock up on to the Dock, roped it up and killed it in the old pole axe manner; in the darkness they bled the animal into the ebb tide and then by lamplight they cut the carcass up in the hold. Next they went up to Wilford Bridge and woke up the crews of three of Parker's barges, which were laying there with cargoes of stone, and sold them meat. The same was done in the Ferry Dock and by dawn every barge in the upper reaches of the Deben had parts of the missing animal hidden aloft in their tops'ls.

Strange to say this crim was never detected, although the police must have had a shrewd idea of what became of the bullock. The following mid-day they entered the 'Boat Inn' and began questioning all barge men and riverside workers who were in there playing coyetts; one constable was even reputed to have remarked that he could smell an extremely good joint in the oven. Never did such an obvious clue get overlooked.

Sometime early in this century Captain Robert Skinner began to play a part in the maritime affairs of Woodbridge. He had been master of the large schooner barges *Zebrina* and *Belmont* which were owned by the Whitstable Shipping Co. Then Skinner started on his own as part owner of the boomie *Lord Alcester* with the coal merchant Cox. The Deben was a good place to establish a barge owning enterprize. After all, there was no one else attempting it. Skinner's method of retailing coal was to sell it straight out of the barge in small amounts. It was easier for the village people to buy it at riverside quays than to collect it from Woodbridge or Melton stations. Word went round when Skinner was in the river and anyone wanting coal took a horse and tumbrel or even just a wheelbarrow down to the waterside to buy some.

The *Lord Alcester* used to bring 290 tons up to The Jetty at Woodbridge. Skinners next acquisition was the boomie *Lord Hartington* which worked into the Suffolk estuaries. However, the Depression of the 1920's went against this attempt to build up a fleet of sailing barges. *Lord Alcester* was sold and was later lost running into Poole and the *Lord Hartington* was run down by a German cargo liner in the River Schelde in 1928. Next Skinner bought the *Dover Castle* and the *Tuesday,* both of which were small rather old sprities.

Captain Skinner's three sons went into his barges. John skippered the *Lord Hartington* until he took a job in North Woolwich, Wesley was mate with his father in the *Lord Alcester* and later owned the *Martin Luther* and *Nautilus.* George, the youngest of this sea going family, first 'went away' in the *Zebrina* when she was rigged as a barquentine. Later he came back to Woodbridge to help with the family coal business, but could not settle and went off again, into steamers. He became a quarter-master in the P & O lines and then changed to the continental ferry service from Harwich before he came back to barges. He even took the *Dover Castle,* which was not a coasting barge, up to the Humber after coal but preferred taking *Lord Alcester* with coal from the Tyne to the Biscay ports. This barge carried five hands and an average passage took nine or ten days. After this he went as skipper in Cranfield's Ipswich grain barges, having the *Venture* for quite a while, but he did not like spritty barges; they were never out of the sight of land for long enough.

The last work Captain Robert Skinner could find for his barges was to carry shingle up from the Deben bar for building material. This really was flogging a dead horse, since every vessel has to earn its own replacement value & shingle carrying barely gave a living wage. It did not even keep the *Tuesday* in good order; she drifted up and down on the tide with sails in pieces. It must have been a sad blow for the old Captain. He had played an important part in the development of the sailing barge and had commanded some of the very finest craft back in the 1890's. But he did not give up, infact he died, aged 82, aboard the *Tuesday off* Green Point in 1935. After that, Woodbridge Ferry Dock was full of laid-up barges.

No one can remember when the last barge discharged a cargo at Woodbridge. The *Nautulus* lay in the Ferry Dock for years and was finally sold for a house boat at Pin Mill. *Eureka* also lay there, perhaps there was some idea of converting her to a yacht. I do not know. Mr. Carr had the barge *Edith Mary* here as a yacht, and after this he bought the tops'l schooner *Isabella,* a pointed stern vessel built in Lancashire and totally unsuitable for the East Coast. After the war this schooner went to the Hamble River as a houseboat.

In these last days of Woodbridge's history as a port Horlock's steel barge *Repertor* was almost sunk at the Tide Mill Quay. Barges with their flat bottom were rather prone to creating suction in the mud which prevented them from floating with the tide. It did not often happen, although Hythe Quay Colchester is noted for it. In the case of the *Repertor,* her skipper was just turning in for the night when he noticed that the barge was not rising with the tide. As quickly as possible they put the hatches on and caulked up all the deck openings. The usual methods of breaking the suction were tried, but it was not until the deck was under water up to the bottom of the wheel that *Repertor* suddenly lurched up and shook herself free of the mud

What remained of the town's trade was left to the steamers. The first steamer ever seen here was the *George & Jane* in the May of 1834 and a few years later an attempt was made with the *Eclipse* to start a regular service to London, but this was withdrawn in 1842. Small steamers came in often but were never really at home in the river. The 196 gross tons *River Witham* came here regularly in the early 1930's but it was Dutch coasters that brought the last freights of dried peas to Woodbridge Canning Co's Warehouse at Sun Wharf, right up to 1939. The port never progressed after this, it really died with the age of sail.

The traditions of coastal sail are particularly strong on the East Coast. A man who typified this dogged determination not to give in to powered craft was Captain William Kirby. Although he was a member of a well known Bradwell barging family he must have known the Deben as well as his native Essex estuaries for he traded up to Wilford Bridge for many years. He was skipper in Parker's fleet and he married a Bromeswell girl and set up home there. His first barge was the *Daisy Maud* and after that the famous racing barge *Veronica.* He then took the *Duchess* and with her he must have brought hundreds of tons of Kentish stone for the East Suffolk County Council's road making depot at Wilford Bridge. This was looked on by bargemen as being a fairly easy trip. Harold Smy used to go up in the *Eldrid Watkins* and he told me that the real secret was having two good pilots, Ted Marsh and Nelson Oxborrow.

Captain Kirby, nicknamed 'Admiral Truthful', appears to have been a tough nut. Once he got drunk at Maldon and his fellow skippers, who had a very down to earth sense of humour, locked him up in the mortuary. When 'Willum' Kirby came to he discovered that the only comfortable place to sleep was in a coffin, so he moved its occupant out and slept in it for the rest of the night.

At the beginning of the Second World War, *Duchess* was fitted with a small gun on the foredeck. Off Harwich one night, Captain Kirby heard enemy aircraft coming in overhead, so he decided to let them have it with his armament. The German aircraft flew on undamaged, but he succeeded in shooting away a great deal of the barge's gear. Shortly after this he took the *Duchess* to the Dunkirk evacuation and had to leave her on the beach. Kirby then took Wakley Bros' *Water Lily*.

By then it was obvious that sailing barges were no longer a commercial proposition. Even the Essexmen were having a job to keep them going and most of the barges were being motorized. One day the dreaded order came; the *Water Lily* was to have an engine put in. Kirby had no use for a smelly diesel engine in his cabin. He did not understand them. He was then 72 years old and the worry brought on a stroke. After three days in bed he departed to Pin Mill and although he had lost the use of one arm he sailed *Water Lily* to London. It was his last trip. The days of sail only had finished. There was no point in going on.

CHAPTER 7

YACHTS OF THE RIVER DEBEN

IN June of 1783 the *Templer* and the *Flora* raced from Woodbridge to Bawdsey Ferry and back for a 'valuable silver' cup. After this there was a lunch at the 'Queen's Head'. The event got some publicity because some unsporting character stole one of the contesting craft. There was quite a fuss about this but it looks as if the craft was eventually returned. Whether this race was between yachts or passenger carriers is not certain. However it does appear to be the first mention of racing on the Woodbridge River. Racing of one sort or another has been going on more or less continuously ever since.

The Deben Yacht Club was founded in 1830 and by then there was a small nucleus of yachts kept on moorings off the Ferry Dock. Some of these were the *Rival, Syren* and the *Pearl*. About the same time the *Helen* made a cruise to Holland from Woodbridge. The shipbuilders must have been responsible for many of the yachts, William Taylor built the *Osprey* and others, no doubt. Garrard built a six oared galley for 'gentlemen to row'. Rowing was a popular pastime until after the First World War and featured quite prominently in the Woodbridge Regatta. In 1854 there was a £3 purse for the winner of skiffs of 18 feet, while the four oared boats shared a purse of 10 sovereigns, seven for the first and three for the second, which suggests that the numbers entered were not very large.

The method of handicapping yachts in the same regatta was to give half a minute for every ton over 12 tons. In the small class the same system was used for every ton above six tons. The yachts competed for a purse of 10 sovereigns, plus 5s. added by the Deben Yacht Club. All very simple, but I have no doubt there were arguments! In the evening there was a dinner at the Crown Hotel, then a fete and fireworks display on the Crown Bowling Green. In 1872 the annual river event was enlarged and called the Grand Woodbridge Regatta, and afterwards there were still the usual festivities in the town. The Deben Yacht Club then appeared to be administering the Regatta and were also holding sailing and rowing matches frequently.

Edward FitzGerald is the 19th century yachtsman we know most about. He was a yachtsman in the Victorian meaning of the word. Not actually taking part in the sailing of the boat; this was done by 'paid hands' with a professional skipper at the wheel who made the decisions. FitzGerald was, to all intents and purposes, a passenger. He owned nine different craft at various times, the best known being the 14 ton schooner *Scandal* which was built at Wivenhoe in 1863 (Woodbridge was at a low ebb at that time, only

The barge yacht 'Esnia' after launching from the Lime Kiln Yard, 1911.

*Woodbridge from the air, 1957. Note the Tide Mill Pond
before it was turned into a yacht harbour.*

Ramsholt Dock, c. 1895. Chicory malting (right) and Dock farmhouse, now the Ramsholt Arms.

Launching of Whisstock's 16 ton ketch ' Landfall' on 27th June, 1960.

boat building was being done). Eight years later *Scandal* was sold to Sir Cuthbert Quilter.

It may seem odd that yachting in the Deben should have been led by two men with such widely different personalities. FitzGerald, the brilliant if slightly unstable, literary gentleman called his yacht after what he considered was Woodbridge's main product. Quilter was the pillar of the local establishment, a much respected and very capable man, but he lacked Fitz-Gerald's humour and changed the schooner's name to *Sapphire*. Not that it made any difference, she was still a wonderful sailer and is known to have been still afloat in 1928.

Quilter also took into his service the *Scandal's* master, Captain Ablett Passiful. This yachtmaster went on to command a long line of craft for Quilter. The largest were the 110 ton *Foam* and the 171 ton *Zoe*. In the seasons of 1874-5, Passiful took the yawl *Hirondelle* round the coast, racing in all the large regattas. Later he commanded the steam yachts *Firefly* and *Peridot*. The registered home port for these yachts was Cowes (which was the correct place for a gentleman to keep his yacht) but they spent quite a lot of time laying in the Deben off Bawdsey Manor. When Quilter represented South Suffolk in the House of Commons, the 43 T. M. ton *Peridot* often lay in the Thames and many prominent statesmen joined him on his steam yacht for a voyage to Bawdsey. No doubt Bawdsey Manor made a welcome sight from the elegant *Peridot* when she rounded Walton-on-the-Naze with black smoke pouring out of her slender funnel.

When the weather was not suitable, or time was pressing, Quilter went up river and caught the train at Woodbridge. The *Peridot* drew six feet of water and was sometimes held up in the upper reaches so that the term 'caught the train' is not quite correct. In fact the station master kept it waiting until Quilter arrived. There was even a special gate made so that he could reach the platform easily.

After Quilter's death *Peridot* was registered in his wife's name until 1919, then the yacht was owned by Maritime Salvors Ltd., of Cowes, where she had been built 25 years before. For the most part this type of very grand yachting was never really part of the Deben scene, although a number of local gentlemen laid their yachts up at Woodbridge from time to time. Best remembered ar Major Miller's *Vibernia* which drew 10ft. and Sir George Manners steam yacht which he kept off Methersgate for a number of years.

The revival of wooden boat building at Woodbridge began when Ebenezer Robertson took over the Lime Kiln Yard. Also known as 'Khartoum' Robertson, he was of Scots descent and wore the kilt and played the bagpipes when he felt so inclined. He already had the St. Peter shipyard at Ipswich where he built barquentines (*Uncle Ned* of 1867 was still afloat at the Arklow in 1940) and boomie barges.

The boomie *Ninita* that he built in 1880 nearly paid for herself in two years but after this there was rather a slump in barges and Ebenezer changed over to yachts. Lime Kiln yard was bought in 1884 to develop the yacht building site, although barges were repaired here. Ebenezer sold Taylor's old patent slip to a Rochester firm and removed the grids where large vessels had previously come up for scrubbing. Every Monday he came by train from Ipswich to inspect the progress at the Lime Kiln and then went on to Southwold where he had property.

Ebenezer's son A. V. Robertson came over to Woodbridge to run the yard when he was 18 and later he was responsible for that curious local phenomenon - the barge yacht. This was an attempt to translate the successes of the large cargo carrying spritties into cruising yachts. The main spring of this movement was the Burnham-on-Crouch yachtsman. E. B. Tredwen. He saw quite correctly that deep keeled yachts were useless for the East Coast and instead pioneered the flat bottomed unballasted barge yacht. The idea rather caught on and a number were built around the East Coast. Robertson made rather a speciality of them. Tredwen had the 25 ft. *Venus* built in which he sailed to the Baltic, the 29 ft. *Nan* in 1904 in which he cruised to Berwick-on Tweed and the 35 ft. *Pearl* which carried a piano and was eventually destroyed by fire on the Clyde.

It was realised that the small boxy gaff rigged barge yachts behaviour left quite a lot to be desired when at sea and that a great part of the spritties success was due to their size. Barge yachts were then built larger, in fact in some cases the same size as trading versions. Howard, the famous Maldon barge builder, produced the 80 ft. *Thoma II* in 1909 and two years later the 40 ft *Lady Frances* for his own use. Robertson's contribution was the lovely *Esnia*. Slightly larger than the *Lady Frances* she was designed by G.U. Laws and built at Lime Kiln yard on a piece of ground just round the corner from the dock. Esnia was spritsail rigged and had what was hoped to be improvements, namely a boom on the mainsail (which cannot have been an improvement) and davits over the leeboards (which must have got in the way considerably).

There must be a great many barge enthusiasts now who would be more than happy to own this lovely little spritty yacht, but she had few admirers then. She was in a class of her own, at least as far as the yachting set were concerned. No owner kept *Esnia* for more than three seasons and she apparently ended up in the Mediterranean. The *Thoma II* also suffered the same fate, her gear being taken out and some kind of ugly deckhouse nonsense shoved in. Barge yachts deserved better treatment than that for, although they are slow, some of them have now been knocking around for over half a century and have still not capsized, as their critics always claimed they would.

The barge yachts were quite popular at Woodbridge because at low tide they would sit on the mud without falling over. A number were kept here including the *Heron*. The last one built here was the 18 ton ketch *Marietta*, in 1916. I remember going on board her in the early 1950's when she was laid up at Waldringfield and being shown the novel 'heads', situated in the bottom drawer of a cupboard in the main saloon. While the *Marietta* was being built at Robertson's the Rev. Will Groom, then a boy at the Woodbridge School, used to go down and watch the progress with admiration. In about 1954 he bought her and put a bermudian mast in her. The *Marietta* caused something of a sensation in early 1967 by sinking at her mooring off Ramsholt Dock on the same day as her owner's death.

Lime Kiln yard was eventually taken on by A. V. 'Robbie' Robertson's son Bert Robertson and during the 1930's they were turning out a 4 ton class boat designed by Capt. O.M. Watts. These cost £175 new and if a Stuart Turner engine was fitted £220. This class which was transon sterned was called the Ranzo, the counter sterned version which was a little more beamy was appropriately known as Mrs. Ranzo. Since Bert Robertson has retired and sold the business, building has stopped at the Lime Kiln yard. By the mid 1960's. A.V. Robertson Ltd., were chiefly concerned with fitting the interior into the fibre glass hulls of the 25 ft. Wing Class.

Robertson's yard proved a training ground for shipwrights and as people have had more money to spend on luxuries so the Woodbridge yacht industry has expanded. When Ebenezer reopened the Lime Kiln yard it was intended that his son-in-law A.A. Everson and son A.V. Robertson should go into partnership, but this did not materialize, so Ebenezer started Everson off as a boat builder on his own, below the Ferry Dock at the Jetty (where Ebenezer also had a coal merchants business) in 1886. In 1923 Everson built the *Dream* an open sailing boat to be hauled up on Aldeburgh beach which is said to have been a copy of a Bombay Tom Tit (whatever they may have been). *Dream* proved popular and later had a cabin fitted. A slightly larger 3 tonner called the *Cherub* was built on the same lines and this proved to be the beginning of a gunter rigged class of yachts suitable for local estuary cruising. The *Cherub's* cost was originally £125 and 24 of these were built by Eversons by 1936. A yacht which may have played a part in influencing the *Cherub* design was the round bowed *Clytie* which was built by Everson in 1922. The round bow made 'going about' at sea difficult and later 6 ft. was added on to her bow and the rig was altered from gaff to bermudian. The *Clytie* has been kept at Everson's Jetty ever since she was built and must be the longest resident yacht kept on the Deben. Every spring, the opening of the sailing season is heralded by the white sailed *Clytie* coming down over the empty grey waters of the Deben on her first weekend cruise. In the autumn when all the other yachts have been laid up, the *Clytie* still sails. When she stops coming, winter really has arrived.

The internal combustion engine had the same revolutionary effect afloat as it did on the roads. The early marine engines were monsters of uncertain temper; quite a number of yachtsmen would have nothing to do with them. Probably the first full powered craft on the Deben was *Monare*. Built in 1902 she was a sort of decked in launch. 'Robbie' Robertson had a similar craft called the *Daimler* with a Daimler engine which dated from roughly the same period and was used for passenger carrying trips. The *Esnia* was fitted with a paraffin Gardener when she was launched in 1909. By the 1920's an 'iron tops'l' was a normal fitting. Many people who were messing about in boats in those far off days have permanent scars as a memorial to the day their primitive engines backfired or exploded in some unexpected manner while they were trying to coach them into life.

For all their uncertainties the combustion engine in small cars gave yachtsmen the opportunity to drive to the anchorages further down the Deben where yachts could lay afloat all the time. What they found were deserted waterside villages and a quiet peaceful estuary. It did not remain that way for long. Waldringfield, since it is the best anchorage and the most pleasant spot, was the first to attract people. A photograph taken around this time shows one small yacht on a calm surface. As the photograph was taken on Whit Monday it is quite possible that the other yacht had gone for a sail down river. Small rowing and dinghy sailing events were held at Waldringfield before the First World War, but the first proper regatta was held in 1920 and the following year the Sailing Club was formed. There was no looking back after that.

Felixstowe Ferry started the same way, a small event every year in which local people and a few holiday makers had sailing and rowing races in heavy clinker dinghies. These eventually blossomed out into what was originally called the Felixstowe Yacht and Dinghy Club. Since then all the clubs on the Deben have linked up to organize Deben Week, when for one week during mid-summer the Deben is covered with sails of every description - white, blue red and yellow, yachtsmen scrambling on their foredecks to dowse their spinnakers and get their big reaching 'gennies' on their craft as the wind direction alters as they go from one reach to another. Dinghies drifting on the tide, their crews quietly waiting for more wind; when it arrives, dinghies the wrong way up with youthful crews bobbing about in the water. Every helmsman hoping, trying to cover himself with glory and his living room shelves with silver cups. There are a lot of people trying, a great many hoping but with so many entrants, not enough glory to go round. Still, there will always be another Deben Week the next year, that you can be sure of.

A unique local custom which has grown up around Deben Week is The Procession which is held on the Sunday at the beginning or end of Deben Week. The bishop of the diocese is taken by boat from some point on the Deben., usually Felixstowe Ferry up to Waldringfield. The bishop's yacht is followed by a procession of flag bedecked yachts, motor cruisers and dinghies. At Waldringfield a Yachtsmen's Service is held on the beach, and a collection is then made by people rowing round the anchored procession fleet. Because it is original and possibly because it only happens once a year, the attendance is usually very good.

With more yachtsmen, there became more work for yacht builders. Nunn Bros., bought the old Waldringfield Cement Factory quay in the early 1920's and began boat building there. The yard is still run by one of the founders 'Ernie' Nunn and has a very good name for dragon class building. They supply owners all over the country. Mike Nunn a younger member of the family, is running Seamark Nunn & Co. at Trimley St. Martin. The tradition of wooden boat construction spread to such an extent that in the 1960's there were nine places in the Deben area where it was possible to have a sizeable boat built.

Unquestionably the best known yard on the Deben is Whisstock's Boat-yard Ltd. Claud Whisstock went to sea in steamships just after the First World War but during the depression it was hard to get a berth on a ship so he did a spell at Robertson's with the object of eventually becoming a ships carpenter and from there he went on to work for Brook Marine at Lowestoft. This job finished abruptly during the 1926 General Strike when Brooks had a 'lock out'. Mr. Whisstock returned to Woodbridge and took on jobs repairing boats but this activity went slowly and his main source of income was from running motor boat trips at the weekends to Felixstowe Ferry and back for 'eighteen pence a head'.

His yard was originally simply a wet marsh near Ferry Dock and the first workshop was built on Stilts. The main point in its favour is that it has 50 yards of frontage on to the Deben. One of the early jobs was patching up the *Nautilus*. This barge was being poked up to Melton Dock when she got stuck on a post in Hackney Reach. As the tide went down, the post came up through the bottom, but as the barges timbers were a bit ripe they did not crack and the post fitted tightly without letting a drop of water in. When Mr. Whisstock and Bow Wilson went up to carry out repairs they found that the post was a piece of witch elm in perfect condition so they sawed off the top and then the bottom outside the barge and told the skipper that it was a far sounder piece of timber than any other in the barge and was best left there.

The first sizeable craft to be built by Whisstock's Boatyard was the 35ft motor cruiser *Bendor* in 1932. After this came the passenger carriers *Ocean*

Viking and *Orwell Viking*. These were followed by a series of Thames launches, lifeboat tenders and any other small vessels built of wood. One of the unusual jobs was to help fit out the full-rigged ship *Joseph Conrad* at Cliff Quay Ipswich in 1934. The whole yard went over and lived aboard this square rigger and later Alan Villiers invited Mr. Whisstock to go as 'chippy' on her world cruise, but by then he had too many ties ashore.

In 1937 the first Deben 4-tonner was launched. These were designed by William Maxwell Blake, a Woodbridge man who had been in charge of a naval dockyard at Hong Kong before he retired to Felixstowe. Until then Woodbridge had relied on London and Burnham-on-Crouch naval architects and had been rather removed from the initial creative force needed for yacht construction. Maxwell Blake did a number of designs during the 30's, notably the *Mirelle*, built by Whisstock's for Philip Allen. As buyers for the Deben 4-tonners were quickly found, Maxwell Blake designed a Deben 6-tonner. Although Whisstocks kept this as a 'stock boat', that is, they did not destroy the moulds or patterns as in the case of a 'one off', only just over half a dozen were built by them. The last Maxwell Blake 'one off' yacht from the yard was *Florence Edith* in 1938. After the war this yacht was bought by Sir Francis Chichester who renamed her *Gipsy Moth* and he learnt to sail in her. Following *Florence Edith* Mr. Whisstock designed the 46 ft. motor cruiser *Reda* which apart from smaller boats constructed on the yard is the only craft designed by him.

By the time the Second World War started Whisstocks had become the prime boat building yard at Woodbridge. The war years saw over 200 craft for various uses built for the War Department, Admiralty and Ministry of Transport. After the war it was not possible to get wood for pleasure craft and the yard concentrated on fishing boats for a time. In 1946 two Deben 4-tonners left the yard and the following year saw a gradual change over to yachts. In 1948 the Deben 4-tonner *Wren* was built for Percy Woodcock and the *Carte Blanch* for Geoffrey Ingram-Smith. By then this class was being sold to owners in the U.S.A., Canada and Spain.

'Jack' Francis Jones of Waldringfield qualified as a naval architect in 1941, but spent the war years in Naval Coastal Forces and was invalided out in 1945. Amongst J. Francis Jones' many designs is the 46 ft 26 ton gaff cutter *Corista*, built by Whisstocks for Philip Allen in 1952. An exceptionally handsome craft with a very bold sheer, she is one of the finest of her type ever produced. In 1963, when *Corista* had already made over 40 North Sea crossings she took part in the first East Coast Old Gaffers Race (old gaff rigged boats sailed by young men) and was easily the first over the finishing line, making an unforgettable sight as she came up Harwich Harbour under full-sail in the moonlight. While taking part in subsequent races which have been held on the Blackwater Estuary, we have been able to see several of the older Woodbridge built yachts trying out their paces. The veteran of these is the Robertson-built *Clytie* of 1913 (the second yacht launched by them with that name). Some of the Everson's Cherubs, the hardy *Sea Pig* built in 1931, the *Spindrift* and the *Jubilee* which must have been one of the last of the class built. Then a couple of Deben 4-tonners *Inanda* and *Reginald The Dane* (how did she get that name?). An interesting yacht is the *Young Alert*. The original *Alert* was built by Dan Hatcher at Southampton in 1855. She spent the war years in a mud berth at Waldringfield and when she was taken to Woodbridge was found to be completely rotten. Every frame on the port side was removed and J. Francis Jones took her lines off and Whisstocks built an exact replica called the *Young Alert* in 1946.

By 1954 the demand for Deben 4-tonners had stopped, 54 had then been completed. Whisstocks did build one more in 1960 though for an American who had lost his original one in hurricane 'Carol'. This one was built of teak and should therefore last indefinitely. In 1956 they built the 4½ ton *Phille* which was the first yacht built to a design by Kim Holman and was for his own use. Five years later a yard stock boat by the same design-er called the Holman 26 (feet) was started and shortly after this another class the H (olman) 50 was begun.

It is very difficult to pick out a pattern, but to begin with Whisstocks built any kind of craft that was needed. Then came the small Deben class, but in recent years fibreglass has completely taken over these smaller classes and the yard is now turning out a variety of larger sailing craft. I quote some of the more recent products. The 'racing machine' *Breeze of Yorkshire* intended for the One Ton Cup, the Maurice Griffiths designed 17 ton ketch *Good Hope* which was balustrading round her high stern and the J. Francis Jones designed 9½ ton diesel ketch *Gingerbread*. Practically the only bare hull which has been brought to this yard for completion was Hammon Innes' *Mary Deare*. She was built of steel in Holland, and brought here for fitting out. The gaff still appeals to some owners on the East Coast, some of the recent Whisstock yachts have had this rig. Dr. Wells' *Fargo* is gaff and so too was the *Alan II* until she came back for a bermudian mainsail in readiness for a voyage to the West Indies.

These yachts are tailor made to fit the individual owners tastes. They are all built of wood. Claud Whisstock says that building yachts is his hobby, he would not have the interest in fibreglass or any synthetic material. Wood is a natural material and is a pleasure to work with. It goes deeper than that. A craftsman building a wooden yacht builds his character into it. No two wooden boats are the same. No two craftsmen are the same. Sisterships built at the same place, at the same time by different men will often handle differently.

The wooden sailing vessel is one of the most beautiful objects mankind has ever conceived, but progress (if it is progress) marches on. The cold hands of economics stretch out over the water and dictate the type of craft that shall float on it. However by 1972 Woodbridge had become practically the last place in Britain where wooden yachts were constructed.

The effect of more people wanting to spend their leisure afloat has one obvious result. More yachts mean more moorings which in turn leaves less room for an increasing number of craft to manoeuvre. The situation, however unavoidable, is similar to that of the mythical bird which flew round in ever decreasing circles. The days of peace and quiet on the estuaries of the East Coast are gone. Any one wanting to 'get away from it all' is advised to get well out to sea. Manoeuvring in a crowded estuary is no place for relaxation. Problems of crowding, which basically come down to too many people living on one island, are of course far more acute ashore than afloat. The story of Ramsholt is a classic of the East Coast - a deserted barge quay at the end of a lane full of potholes and a handful of local yachtsmen. If you went into the pub Mrs. Nunn invited you to go down the cellar and get your own beer from the barrel. More than six people in the bar was a crowd to be remembered. In the dark evenings the clock ticked away, the Tilley lamp hissed and gave out a gentle yellow light and an elderly waterman George Cook sat in the corner drinking mild from 'his' brown mug.

Visitors occasionally came and plonked themselves down in George's corner (it had the only view of the river) and the atmosphere always became tense until the offender realised his mistake and moved. Once a smart yacht got ashore on the mud and its crew who were not entirely sure what they were trying to do hailed 'Cooky' for assistance. Off he went wearing his farm workers hob nailed boots; these permanently marked the laid teak deck. He then lost his favourite clay pipe overboard and in the mounting confusion he fell through the cabin skylight. He was not really to blame for any of these, but as he said later 'that was the w'erry devil'. He bore the summer visitors no grudge, they kept his brown mug filled for years, but if they did start to throw their weight around he had only to light up his 'clay' with his home grown tobacco (which was just the job for breaking in clay pipes) and they quickly departed for the purer air of the nearest town. His 'mixture' which gave off a curious blue haze brought tears to the eyes and even made one or two of the locals gasp for breath. In spite of inhaling this he lived to be a very old man, but the peaceful scene he knew through out his life passed into history in the mid-1950's - the Deben had been discovered.